CULTURE CHANGERS

CULTURE changers
RECONNECTING HIS FAMILY

To Ali,
with love + blessings

From John & Margaret. xxx

GINNY CRYER

I read this book + thought
of you. :) ∠ xxx

ISBN: 978-1505593129

© Copyright 2014 Ginny Cryer

Published by Culture Changers   www.culture-changers.org

Published using KWS services. www.kingdomwritingsolutions.org
Some of the material contained in this book was previously
published as 'Introducing Culture Changers' and "Culture-Changers
– Reconnecting His Family" ISBN: 978-1-907080-37-1

Cover & Interior Design and Formatting by Lorraine Box and Max
Randall

Culture Changers is a Charitable Company, Registered in England
and Wales. Company No. 8268325 and Charity No. 1152979.

DEDICATED TO

Hugh

Who shows me what it is to be loved
by a truly godly and inspirational husband.
A man to whom ungodly control is anathema.
It is my honour and delight
to walk this road alongside him.

My Family

Especially to my parents,
Reggie and Juliet Llewelyn,
who inspired me to follow my own dreams.
My father had a heart for prison reform.
He memorably said
"Every person, however bad,
has inside them a spark of hope!
It is our job to find that spark
and be a match to it, setting it on fire,
creating opportunity for change."

PREFACE

I clearly remember the first time I met Hugh and Ginny. They are a quintessential English couple, steeped in everything I love about my country. Their accents, their history, and their love of England are evident to all. In the same way, they are a quintessential revival couple. Everyone who knows them, or hears their story, is attracted to them and the King whom they so faithfully represent. What Ginny has written manages to embrace so many deep and life changing truths, and yet it is easily digestible. If you know their story, you will have heard how Ginny, when first touched by God, exclaimed to Hugh in her beautiful accent, "My darling, I think we've got it." I for one can confirm that they have, and now they are sharing it with us all.

Paul Manwaring
Global Legacy, Bethel Church, Redding, California

A NOTE FROM HUGH

As a family, we became followers of Jesus, not for social reasons but because we were in rather a mess! We give comfort with the comfort we have received and having begun to be restored, we believe Jesus hinted to us that He wanted Ginny and me to take our part in restoring His Family too. Since that time some 30 years ago, our lives have been a journey of discovery as we have sought to live the sort of life about which we read in the New Testament. "Doing the stuff" as John Wimber would say, not just talking about it! For nearly thirty years we have had a passion for seeing the Kingdom of God come through small gatherings and we have felt most at home in these more intimate settings.

We have moved house four times in response to what we believe was His call on our lives for a particular season. Each time has been the next step of faith and always an eventual blessing. Over the years we have visited France, Germany, Africa, Russia and Siberia seeking the Kingdom together. There has always been a blessing of giving and impartation on each visit. As hungry believers we have also been invited to North America for further personal equipping – for which we are enormously grateful.

We planted the Winchester Vineyard in 1994. A good year! As time went by, we felt God saying that the "Winvin" looked better than it was! In our attempts to shore up some of the areas of our weakness, the Lord brought across our path some amazing new friends to help us. Firstly we embraced "Jesus Ministry", then the "Father Heart" message – which was life–changing for us both – and then we began to be impacted by some of the teaching coming from Bethel Church in Redding, CA. Each of these equipping seasons brought fresh and further revelation to build on what we had already been doing and further strengthening our foundations.

As our time leading the Winchester Vineyard drew to a close, we felt God reminding us again of his desire to see His Family become One and part of that was for us to pioneer "Culture Changers." We are at present establishing small gatherings across the United Kingdom and in other nations when invited. From these gatherings we are meeting those with whom we are sharing our new vision. Some are welcoming the Culture

Changers blueprint and framework which enables them to meet together with friends and colleagues as led by the Holy Spirit. We now have a slightly better idea of what we are doing, but the full extent is  only slowly unfolding and we are excited to be on this journey and are grateful for those of you who are pleased to walk with us. Although Ginny and I are involved in this together, this book is entirely her work..

Hugh Cryer

ACKNOWLEDGEMENTS

On our journey, Hugh and I have been honoured to meet and learn from some of the fathers and mothers in the Church of today who have shared their lives with us. It is partly from these saints, and the messages they each carry, that we are being chiselled and shaped ourselves.

We are indebted to **John Wimber**, founder of the *Vineyard Movement*, and to **John and Eleanor Mumford**, leaders of the UK Vineyard, who taught us how to pioneer and take some of our first Kingdom steps.

To the Winchester Vineyard, the church we planted and love so much – what an adventure we had, as together we worked out some of the ways of doing church differently.

To John and Carol Arnott who introduced us to our Heavenly Dad in a much deeper way – and loved us through a time of great trial.

To Mike and Cindy Riches who showed us simplicity with power and brought the revelation of supernatural royalty alive to us from scripture.

To Randy Clark who prayed for me with great power. After that life changing experience the Lord apprehended me for this new work.

To Mark Stibbe for his friendship, encouragement and theological input - and also for agreeing to write a chapter for this book entitled A Culture Changing View of the Cross. We see this message as vital, enabling the fatherless to recognize the true character of their Heavenly Dad.

To Bill Johnson and **Bethel Church** who have shown us what a renewed mind can look like.

To Danny Silk whose message on the *Culture of Honour* is foundational to our vision for the market place.

To Paul and Sue Manwaring who are pioneering a new wineskin and have believed in us as we answered the call to move further outside the box ourselves.

To Steve and Wendy Backlund whose teaching and encouragement enabled us to see things from a higher perspective.

To Faith Blatchford for encouraging me to write this book in the first place. Hugh and I greatly value her friendship and her input into our lives. I am so grateful to her for agreeing to write a chapter for this book entitled Culture and the Sound of Heaven.

We thank them all for their friendship, inspirational obedience, courage and resilience as they model what it is to be a pioneer.

I also want to thank those who have contributed to this second edition, or whom I have quoted:– *Bill Johnson, Jonathan Bugden, Paul Manwaring, Steve and Wendy Backlund, David Pytches, Paul Golf, Isobel Allum, Jeremy and Yvette Britton, Jonathan Cavan, Lance Wallnau, George Barna, Wolfgang Simson and Bob Goff* – some of whose websites you can access from the Resource Chapter later in this book.

My thanks also to Tony and Bryony Yelloly for their help, wisdom, kindness and support as they answered my many questions about the Quaker Movement to which they belong.

I am greatly indebted to *Jonathan Bugden* for his editorial help with this book. Also to *Lorraine Box* and *Max Randall*, my graphic designers who have stood with me in this adventure – thank you. Lastly, I am so grateful to my friend, Kate Tyrrell, for proofing this manuscript.

ENDORSEMENTS

Hugh and Ginny are championing the messages of the amazing Grace of Jesus, the revelation of the Father's heart of love and the Friendship and power of the Holy Spirit (2 Corinthians 13:14). When they walk in these things, lives and cultures are invaded by the Kingdom of Heaven.

John and Carol Arnott
Catch the Fire, Toronto

I recommend this book, enthusiastically, to all those seeking to find a re-creation of God's family on earth.

Anne Watson
UK

I enthusiastically recommend to you Hugh and Ginny Cryer. Their passion for God, heart for His Kingdom, and love for His Church keep them young and encountering fresh revelation.

Mike Riches
Pastor, Founder of Sycamore Commission, and author of
Living Free-Recovering God's Design for Your Life

If revival transforms communities, reformation transforms cultures. Many are praying for a new reformation today. If you're looking for a blueprint for that, I can't think of a better book than this. Ginny's passionate proposal for a church that needs to be Father-focused and family-shaped is foundational. Start with these values and it won't be long before you impact the seven mountains of culture with the irresistible love of Jesus.

Dr Mark Stibbe
Published Author, Script Doctor and leader of
Kingdom Writing Solutions

We have a Heavenly Father who values relationship above all else, and Hugh and Ginny are revealing His heart. Ginny's insights about how the Church will gain a foothold in every area of society are absolutely essential for seeing the Kingdom come on earth as it is in Heaven. They both possess a true heart for mothering and fathering and that is evidenced by the supremacy they place on relationship as the foundation for a thriving Church.

Steve Backlund
Igniting Hope Ministries

I really enjoyed this book. I think it indeed will change cultures and cause people to rethink how we do church. Thanks for answering the call.

Wendy Backlund
Igniting Hope Ministries

Endorsements

From the first call of God on their lives Hugh and Ginny have been on a journey of encounter and revelation. In this book Ginny clearly sets out their vision that the Church is a family and each member is called to be a Culture Changer, bringing Heaven's atmosphere in every sphere of life. This revelation will be an inspiration to the Church in these days.

David and Ruth Hadden
All Nations Church, Leicester

What Ginny has written manages to embrace so many deep and life changing truths, and yet it is easily digestible.

Paul Manwaring
Global Legacy, Bethel Church, USA

I love this book! It really resonated with everything in my heart and contained all the things we are seeking to communicate and put in practice here at River Church and especially through our Leadership Training course where we can model these values in a more intentional way. I believe it will not only be a blessing to everyone who reads it but also a fresh framework for others.

Diana Chapman
River Church, Thames Valley.

Hugh and Ginny carry a childlike passion and enthusiasm for more of God. They honour the richness of their spiritual legacy, but refuse to be shaped by the past. Heaven's realm on earth is their pursuit. "Culture changers' accurately describes their lives and ministries as they have embraced internal cultural change with humility and tenacity. Ginny's book communicates a refreshing appeal to the reader to join with them in their journey – the embracing of Heaven's culture and the joyful release of it into all the earth!

Ian and Marj Rossol
All Nations Centre, Leicester

This book is a manifesto for a new wine skin. A hungry pursuit of heaven's realities has led Hugh and Ginny onto a 'road less travelled', asking questions which challenge deeply held ideals and paradigms with a rare display of both courage and humility. They are a true example of an apostolic mother and father to the British Church, and I pray that this book will open your appetite to greater things yet to come!

Paul Golf
E5 Church, Bristol

Ginny Cryer is clearly a strong Christian leader. The mission statement of Culture Changers sets out an attainable goal that through meeting and interacting in God's name, a community characterised by values of love, respect, encouragement, honesty and forgiveness can reach out to and enrich individuals and further the Kingdom by its example. This inspirational book explains and gives guidance on the realisation of this estimable goal.

Martin Savage
Emeritus Professor of Paediatric Endocrinology, University of London. Coordinator of the Health Care, Science and Research Group at Holy Trinity Brompton, London.

TABLE OF CONTENTS

INTRODUCTION

A Background To Our Vision

At the beginning of his gospel Luke writes: "*Many have undertaken to draw up an account of the things that have been fulfilled (surely believed) among us... Therefore since I myself have carefully investigated... it seems good to me to also write an orderly account for you*" Like Luke, I too felt the Lord prompting me to write this book – the purpose of which is to share our vision for Culture Changers – Kingdom not Christendom.

Our vision began in 1987, when the Lord unexpectedly spoke the words "Families for Christ" to us. He also said that we were to "get up and go into the city and He would then tell us what to do next" – Acts 9:6. This we did! It meant moving up to London to join the Vineyard Movement in the UK. In 1994, after seven years in London, we were released to plant our "own" church in Winchester. The church we loved and served for 17 years. In 2011 we heard the Lord speak to us again saying "Culture Changers."

Therefore we appointed our successors and followed the Lord's call to us to go to a place we did not know – the Midlands in the heart of England.

This transition was successful – both the handover of the church and our move to Warwickshire. For us, it was also a time of blind obedience as we stepped into a new future. Six weeks later, Father supernaturally laid a physical Allen key on my shoulder. This was cool! Amazed, we were led to Isaiah 22:22 where we read that there was a precedent for this – *"I will place on his shoulder the key to the house of David, what he opens no–one can shut, and what he shuts no–one can open"* (NIV). As we stared at the key, we had a sense that it was to symbolise His desire to see *His Family reconnected.*

What followed rocked our world. He showed us that, although He is moving powerfully within many movements in the established churches, He is also calling out hundreds and thousands of His children from these churches as He knew they "no longer fitted there." As part of His plan to see His Church to be *one*, we believe He now is showing us a way to bring connectivity to followers of Jesus – wherever and however they "worship." This family model of the gathering together of His people – *a family without walls* – is not to compete with the "local church." Matthew 9:17 (NIV) expresses our heart well: *"Neither do men pour new wine into old wineskins... No, they pour new wine into new wine-skins, **and both are preserved."***

We believe that we are called to pioneer gatherings of believers who come together through relationships, without hierarchy or pulling rank – a flat network with Holy Spirit leading the way. We see believers just "doing life" together – family life centred around biblical values where Jesus builds His Church in our midst. From this safe place, those of us who are *Culture Changers* can bring the culture of Heaven to earth wherever we live and work – powerfully changing the atmosphere around us to that of love, acceptance, truth, mercy, faithfulness, honesty, purity, integrity and all the fruits of Holy Spirit! As children of God, we seek to enjoy authentic loving relationships with one another and then to give that love away. We seek to be one with Him and one with each other, connected together by Holy Spirit. Our Dad doesn't want us to pick sides but pick Him! Our foundation and plumb–line for everything is relationship. Relationship with God and relationship with one another. Discipleship therefore being the natural overflow as we just do life together in this family environment – simply learning from, and sharing with, one another.

Much of this book is my dream and I am comforted by Philippians 2: 12 as Paul writes *"not that I have already obtained all this, or have already arrived at my goal, but I press on to take hold of that for which Christ Jesus took hold of me".*

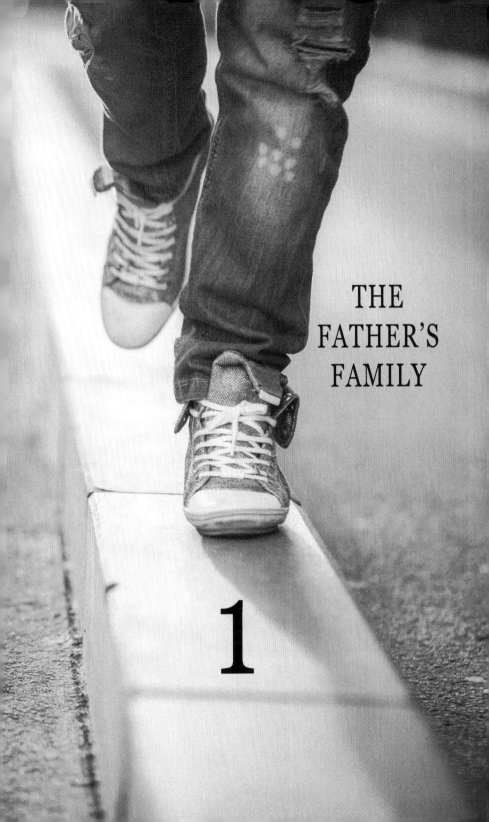

THE
FATHER'S
FAMILY

1

Chapter One

THE FATHER'S FAMILY

The Trinity Models To Us
How Families Can Relate On Earth

Before the earth was made the Father, Son and Holy Spirit were already bound together in a perfect loving relationship, living in absolute certainty of their purpose and honouring one another's differences. In essence they demonstrate true Oneness to us. The Government of Heaven is God the Father, God the Son and God the Holy Spirit. Three in one. So perfect in their loyalty to each other, so perfect in their honour for each other, so perfect in their understanding of the purpose of each other, so secure in the identity of each one, that you can glance at the three and think you only saw one. They are three in one and one in three. They are relationship defined in absolute perfection.[1]

God in His love planned for Adam and Eve to

demonstrate the oneness of the Trinity through the context of a family – so that others may know the same love that exists between Father, Son and Holy Spirit. In Genesis 1:26 God said, *"Let us make man in OUR image, in OUR likeness ..."* and they did! There followed a beautiful time of family relationship – which was only lost when Adam and Eve rebelled. The Bible is the story of God's redemptive mission to get his children back again!

In Genesis 11:7 God says "Come let **US** go down". Equally in Isaiah 6:8 He says "Whom shall I send and who will go for **US**". Note that He says "us" and not "me!" I suggest that God the Father, God the Son and God the Holy Spirit were talking about themselves more as a community of three rather than a remote Heavenly Board with God the father as Chairman. Notice there is an absence of hierarchy although leadership is not in doubt!

GOD'S FAMILY ON EARTH

God has always loved His Family – The Trinity giving us a model of oneness to follow. They long for us to have the same relationship here on earth as they have with each other in Heaven. This is clear from Jesus' prayer in John 17. They long for us to be a family where we are not only brothers and sisters **in** Jesus but also brothers and sisters **of** Jesus. (*John 20:17 Go instead to my brothers and tell them, "I am returning to my Father and your Father, to my God and your God."*).

8

We are called to be a part of a relational family, governed by love rather than rules. A place to include those who find themselves outside the camp (Hebrews 13:13-14). A place where we learn to honour, value, encourage and bravely confront one another in an accepting environment. Just as the early followers of Jesus gathered together in their homes and enjoyed a replica of the Heavenly fellowship Jesus had known before He came to earth, we too can enjoy the same. We can experience being loved and accepted, and be devoted to one another in meaningful relationships. This is God's plan for us as His Family on earth.[2] (If you want to know more about following Jesus then have a look at Appendix One).

With this fresh understanding, we begin to see the church as the joyful gathering of His children – a family without walls or hierarchy. We are fathers, mothers, brothers and sisters, sons and daughters – one big family sharing our lives with one another – with all that that entails. As we enjoy this family relationship with each other we become "the body and bride" that Jesus is longing to return for.

GOD WANTS HIS FAMILY BACK!

In 1987, my husband, Hugh and I felt The Lord talk to us about His longing to see His family reconnected. He then gave us further confirmation in 2012 that He wanted His family back – not just His Church! The Apostle Paul wrote in Ephesians 1:10 that the purpose of God is to: *"bring all things in Heaven and on earth together under one head, even Christ."* We found ourselves catapulted into new ways of thinking. We looked to see how the early followers of Jesus met together as a family modelled on the relationship between our Heavenly Dad, Jesus and the Holy Spirit – functioning in the same loving and submissive way.

In doing so, we believe the Lord unfolded to us a new framework where these family relationships are expressed and worked out in a rather different way from that which we may have experienced before. A framework where people are transformed as they experience being forgiven, adopted into God's family, discipled, loved and accepted. Where we are known as a son or daughter, without a need to perform or prove ourselves. A perfect setting where the weak and the lonely, the widow and the orphan may happily settle and be defended; their need for family being at least as great as their need for protection and provision. Our "template" is taken from Acts 2:42 - 47 where a functional family is nurtured by loving parental authority (1 Thessalonians 2:7 and 11; Philippians 2:22)

Many followers of Jesus are looking for genuine relationships where they can explore new ways of being "family" together. They are seeking an expression of church that is not institutionally based where everyone can take their place, with a function but not a status. In the Culture Changers family there is no hierarchy. John Wimber, the Father of the Vineyard Movement, used to say "Everyone Gets To Play" – meaning that we all get to do the things that Jesus did! The Bible calls this "the priesthood of all believers" as each one can play their part in healing the sick, setting the captives free and – yes – raising the dead. Power is part of the gospel and should be part of our everyday lives.

As in any family, there is leadership, but this is given through relationship, commitment to one another, and trust. Just as in an extended family, there will also be those with more experience in some areas than others. The Five Fold Ministry emerges where different facets of Jesus are represented through servant leadership. Our common bond is our quest for deeper intimacy with our Heavenly Father, Jesus and the Holy Spirit and to equip His Family.

EndNotes

1 Paul Manwaring
2 Acts 2:42

RECONNECTING
HIS
FAMILY

2

Chapter Two

RECONNECTING HIS FAMILY

We cannot talk about reconnecting the family of God without considering the Jewish people and the nation of Israel. I know that this is a controversial issue, but sooner or later we have to realize that at least as far as the Apostle Paul was concerned, the church was always designed by God to be a family in which divided races were united. The most divided races of all were of course the Jews and the Gentiles. Jews and Gentiles did not get on in Paul's day. At best there was often suspicion in both directions. At worst there was outright prejudice and hatred. Tensions between the two ran very high.

In light of this we have to understand how radical it was on the Day of Pentecost when Peter, a Jew by race, stood up and proclaimed that the Holy Spirit had now been poured out on **all** flesh. No longer was the *Ruach ha Kodesh* (the Holy Spirit) reserved for a few people in

Israel. Now the Holy Spirit could be received by anyone who called on the name of Jesus, including Gentiles. From this point onwards, the church was to be a Spirit-filled family in which there was no hint of ageism, classism, sexism and especially racism. God's family was to have a unity that astounded the world and confounded the devil.

A SUPERNATURAL FAMILY

This vision of a supernaturally united family is precisely what we find worked out in the life of the Apostle Paul. He was a Jew; in fact, he claims that he was the very epitome of what it meant to be a good Jew. That meant keeping Gentiles at arm's length. The Gentiles were *ha goyim*, pagans. They were the great unclean. Yet after Paul met the Risen Jesus on the Damascus Road, all that changed. Now this fervent Jew becomes the Apostle to the Gentiles! Baptized in the Holy Spirit, he was the one who went courageously to the non-Jew to woo them into God's saving embrace through the preaching of the Gospel of Peace. That is some transformation, I think you'll agree!

GETTING RECONNECTED

Paul's vision of the church is therefore an astonishing one. He regards the church as a family where there are no longer racial divisions because Jews and Gentiles have together confessed that Jesus is *ha mashiach* (the Messiah). Through Christ both Jews and Gentiles have access to Abba Father through the Holy Spirit, who has made one united people out of two divided races (Ephesians 2:18). This is a miracle! God's family has been reconnected. Jews and Gentiles worship *Abba* Father together, in the same gathering, sharing in the same *shalom* or 'peace.'

A MIRACULOUS RECONCILIATION

From Paul's perspective, one of the keys to such a miraculous reconciliation is for Gentile believers in Jesus to understand by revelation of the Holy Spirit their privileges in Christ. One of these privileges is the fact that Gentile believers in Jesus have the priceless honour of no longer being excluded from citizenship in Israel; they are no longer foreigners to the covenants (Ephesians 2:12). Now Gentile followers of Jesus have been engrafted like wild olive branches onto the cultivated olive tree of Israel (Romans 11:11-24).

Sadly, this revelation has frequently been neglected. Too often Gentile Christians have been influenced by 'replacement theology' - the view that the Gentile church has replaced and superseded the people of Israel.

WE ARE CALLED TO LOVE ISRAEL

Sadly, many Gentile Christians - including some of the great heroes of the faith (such as St Augustine and Martin Luther) - have engaged in blatant anti-Semitism, laying the foundations many would argue for the *Shoah*, the holocaust. We believe that this is profoundly wrong.

Gentile followers have not replaced Israel nor are they to hate the Jews. Gentile followers of Jesus have become engrafted into Israel. In Christ, they are part of a family that goes back to Abraham, Isaac and Jacob - the patriarchs whose lives form the roots of the cultivated olive tree. Gentile believers are called to embrace and love Israel, not to exclude her.

A WAKE-UP CALL!

To many of you reading this book, this may feel like a bit of a surprise. Maybe it feels somewhat random, uncomfortable even. Perhaps it will help if I explain the background to why I feel it is so important to share with you our need to wake up over the whole subject of Israel.

It was November 2013 and Hugh and I were about to teach a gathering of believers about the 'unifying building blocks' for Culture Changers. Before we did that, we sensed Jesus saying that there was something missing in our foundations. As we sought The Lord for what this might be, He was quick to answer. He reminded us that our new call is to reconnect His Family. This meant that He didn't want us to overlook or neglect our Jewish roots. He didn't want us to be deaf to His call to love the Jewish people. He wanted us to seek after the New Testament vision of the church as a united family of both Jew and Gentile sons and daughters.

In the past we had rather a 'laissez faire' attitude towards Israel and veered more towards replacement theology. Now we began to understand that as believers from a Gentile background, we needed to be aware of our heritage as the people of God grafted onto the cultivated olive tree that might loosely be called Biblical Judaism.

RENEWING OF OUR MINDS

To be honest, this was a shock and we entered a time of waiting on The Lord for His direction as he recalibrated our thinking and renewed our minds. We were concerned not to go overboard about Israel and yet at the same time we began to see the agony that replacement theology was causing our Father in Heaven and what devastating divisions it was causing on earth.

In light of this, we had to seek His face and study His word, asking the Holy Spirit to show us what we had been missing all these years.

This pursuit caused us to see His family in a fresh way - with minds illuminated by the Holy Spirit.

THE FATHER'S FAMILY

What does it mean for Gentile believers to love the Jewish people and to seek to bring them into the Father's embrace? Does it mean that Gentiles have to become like Jewish people, wearing skull caps and getting circumcised? No!

This is where we believe some Gentile believers can go to extremes and in the process put others off from seeing the goodness of our heavenly Father's inclusive plan.

UNITY NOT UNIFORMITY

Our Father in heaven never wanted uniformity. He wanted unity. In other words, he never commanded us to become indistinguishable from each other. He called us to honour each other.

Most parents do their level best to avoid favouritism in their family. They prefer to value the uniqueness of each child, loving each child with equal affection. How much more is this true of the family of the Trinity in heaven! The love of the Father, the Son and the Holy Spirit honours our uniqueness as human beings. His love calls us into unity not uniformity.

NO RACIAL STEREOTYPES!

Thus there is no need for Gentiles to become Jewish and there is no need for Jews to become Gentiles. We are to be conformed to the image of Jesus, not the image of a racial stereotype!

The Apostle Paul, in his *Letter to the Romans*, has been so illuminating for us in this regard. We gather that initially in Rome the church was made up of both Jew and Gentile believers in Jesus, but that when Claudius expelled the Jews from Rome, the Gentiles got on rather well without them - so well, in fact, that when Priscilla and Aquilla and the other Jews were allowed to return, they found that they were no longer welcome in the church. They wrote to Paul, who then addressed this issue in Romans 9-11, teaching that Gentiles are grafted into God's adopted people, the Israel of God. We therefore come from them, not the other way round. What is more, as Gentiles we can enter into the blessings of Abraham through our Jewish roots.

DISCOVERING OUR JEWISH ROOTS

Hugh and I therefore began to understand that we who are grafted in (Gentile believers in Jesus) receive great blessings as we honour our Jewish roots. We started to understand the Scriptures with new eyes as we studied (and continue to study) the Word from a Hebraic perspective. This has led to us seeing that priceless blessings await us if we are prepared to be those who would change their lenses and recognize the importance of Israel. Indeed, we believe we are called to say with Ruth (the Gentile) the words she spoke to Naomi (the Israelite): 'Your people are now my people.'

ENRICHING NOT ENSLAVING

When the Lord first corrected Hugh and me about not recognising the importance of Israel, we were concerned not to be led into legalism. This was a concern for the Gentiles in the early church too. This is why, with great wisdom and under the illuminating power of the Spirit, the Jewish apostles confirmed that foisting their religious customs on new Gentile believers was not in the Father's plan. This was reinforced in Acts 15 when the Council of Jerusalem brought a wonderful freedom to new followers of Jesus from a Gentile background by refusing to impose their practices, customs and rituals on new Gentile converts.

LEAVING LEGALISM BEHIND

Therefore as followers of Jesus, the Jewish Messiah, we can all leave legalism behind. Our calling is not to be a people under law but a people filled and joined by the Holy Spirit. The genuine mark of being in the New

Covenant and a member of the universal church was and always will be the mark of God's Spirit and that has not changed.

With the Holy Spirit burning in our hearts, we can now honour one another's differences, understanding that our unity as Jewish and Gentile believers is centred on Jesus not on religious laws and rituals. Rather than being blinded by our racial prejudices or by our obsessions with the law, our model is Jesus who demonstrates what the law looks like in practice as He is concerned with the law's greater purpose - that we may learn His ways that will help us to love God and to love others.

THE LAW OF LOVE

Put succinctly, what unites us in the Father's family is the law of love, not the love of law. When the law of love is activated in our hearts, we begin to see the Jewish people as God's adopted people. That hasn't changed. As Paul stated in Romans 9:4, 'theirs is the adoption as sons.' The present tense still holds. The Father has never torn up this certificate of adoption. The nation of Israel is still and will always be His chosen, honoured, adopted son. His covenant of adoption is forever, not merely for a season.

Not only do we see that the Jews are God's adopted people, we see and understand that the Father chose Israel first - in other words, before he chose and adopted

Gentile believers in Jesus. This is why the Apostle Paul preached the Gospel to the Jews first when he went on missions to a city in the ancient world. Paul honoured his own people and sought to awaken them to faith in Jesus, the Messiah, before he appealed to the Gentiles.

THE TIMES ARE CHANGING

Having said that, since the New Testament era we have been in what Jesus called 'the time of the Gentiles.' In other words, we have been in a long stretch of history spanning nearly two thousand years in which it has predominantly been Gentiles who have come to Christ through the preaching of the Gospel. That season, however, came to an end with the miraculous restoration of the Jewish people to *ha aretz*, the Land, in 1947. Since then, more and more Jewish people have come to confess Jesus as Messiah and Lord. Indeed, it is often said that more Jews have become followers of Jesus in the last twenty years than in the previous twenty centuries put together. Clearly the times are changing.

FULFILLING HIS DREAM

What this means is that for the first time in church history the Father's dream of a united family of Jewish and Gentile sons and daughters can truly be fulfilled. Today, more than at any other time in the past, we can hope and pray to see churches where Jews and Gentiles both have access to the same heavenly Dad through Christ and in the one, same Holy Spirit (Ephesians 2:18). What Paul foresaw, in other words, we can see in our day.

For this to happen, Gentile believers in Jesus must not force Jewish believers to become like Gentiles, and Jewish believers in Jesus must not force Gentile believers to become like Jews. If that happens, then the family of God will not be reconnected and the two will become divided not united. We must all resist the enemy, who is a legalist. We must all rebuff the demonic impulse to oppress. Our reconciliation is intended to enrich us, not enslave us.

A TIME TO PRAY

We are called to be a people who love one another no matter what our background or ethnicity; a people who are ready to forgive one another for the misunderstandings, treacheries and even brutalities of the past that we may together change the world around us as glory-carriers throughout the earth; a people, indeed a family, that will stand with Israel in these last days when she may well become completely isolated; a people who know that whatever the outward circumstances, our Father is neither slumbering nor sleeping.

Let's therefore pray that we may honour our Jewish

roots and that those Jews that have hardened their hearts may be provoked to jealousy by our love for their history, their Scriptures and their covenants, not to mention our love for them as people. That way they may be moved to recognize *Yeshua*, Jesus, as their Messiah, as we have.

"REPENTANT HUMANITY"

I have repented of replacement theology and even the anti-Semitism that may have blighted my heart, falling down on my knees in godly sorrow and resolving to renounce all wrong thinking and allow the Holy Spirit to renew my mind. As the great Jewish teacher, Rabbi Soloveitchik, once put it, 'the highest level of human destiny is to be attained not by rational or religious humanity but rather by repentant humanity –' homo penitens.' Only God can do this and He is!

A change of mind leads to a change of heart. As we all step out in faith, not knowing the future but knowing the One who does, we can be reassured by the words of Oswald Chambers that 'gracious uncertainty is the mark of the spiritual life.' Paul's vision of a new humanity made up of Holy Spirit filled Jews and Gentiles worshipping Abba together remains largely unseen. But today more than at any other time in history we come to see with unveiled minds that it is a promise on the cusp of a miraculous fulfilment.

With thanks to the following authors who have helped me on this journey:

- Rob Richards, *Has God finished with Israel?*
- Robert Heidler, *The Messianic Church Arising*
- Don Finto, *Your people are My people*
- David Pawson, *Teaching tapes on Romans 9-11*
- Mark Stibbe, *The Fathers Tears: The Cross and the Father's Love*

CULTURE
CHANGER'S
DNA

3

Chapter Three

CULTURE CHANGER'S DNA

OUR HERITAGE

In 1656 George Fox wrote: "Be patterns, be examples in all countries, places, islands, nations, wherever you come, that your carriage and life may preach among all sorts of people, and to them; then you will come to walk cheerfully over the world, answering that of God in every way." To our astonishment, we began to realise that part of our vision was similar to what was known as the "Advices and Queries" of the early Quakers.[1]

John Wimber, (Vineyard Movement) himself once a leader of the Yorba Linda Friends Church, came to realise that he was conforming to a degree that he was "institutionalising himself and preaching the party line." Therefore he knew he had to leave the Quaker Movement. During this time, he sensed his world view was changing. Previously he had seen life through a rational, materialistic Western world–view. Now, he began to understand "life supra–rationally" and found he was developing a love for the whole church. Denominations no longer mattered to him. He came to love Richard Baxter's maxim "In necessary things, unity; in doubtful things, liberty; in all things charity".[2]

In 2013, after the Lord had called Hugh and me out of denominationalism, we were reminded of our Vineyard and, indeed, earlier Quaker and Calvary Chapel roots. We are very grateful for them all. We believe that the vision the Lord is giving us for **Culture Changers** continues to build on parts of their original vision – that His Kingdom may come on earth as it is in Heaven. In our emerging blueprint we recognise there are some basic similarities from all these Movements.

EVERY FAMILY HAS ITS OWN DNA

We believe that The Lord is showing us some scaffolding we are to put in place as He directs the building of **Culture Changers**. Much of the construction is built around people (living stones) and our focus is therefore about "being" and not "doing." As a flat network, each Family will have its own vision, accountability, resources and, yes, administration with the Scriptures as its manual for life. His love and His ways are the basis of the framework that will surround us all. The soil on which our homes are founded is deeply enriched by His Presence.

From this place of security we reach out to others with the love of God we carry as we are strengthened and encouraged by the Holy Spirit, living in the fear of the Lord" (Acts 9:31).

WHAT WE BELIEVE

- We believe in the love our Heavenly Father has for all His children – His Family. The Apostle Paul writes "For this reason, I kneel before the Father, from whom **His whole family in Heaven and on earth** derives its name" (Ephesians 3:15 NIV).

- We believe in **Jesus Christ and Him crucified** (1 Corinthians 2:2 NIV).

- We believe in Heaven and hell and that **Jesus died for our sins to rescue us from this present evil age** (Galatians 1:3–4 NIV).

- We believe that Jesus is the head of the Church. *"And He made known to us the mystery of His will according to His good pleasure, which He purposed in Christ, to be put into effect when the times will have reached their fulfillment – to bring all things in Heaven and on earth together **under one head, even Christ"*** (Ephesians 1:9–10 NIV).

- We believe in the indwelling, empowering presence of the Holy Spirit and His ability to be our covering

—being more than able to lead us Himself. *"I will ask the Father to send you **another Helper, the Spirit of truth, who will remain constantly with you.**"* (John 14:16 NIV).

- We believe the bible is the Word of God. *"All of Scripture is God–breathed; in its inspired voice, we hear useful teaching, rebuke, correction, instruction and training for a life that is right so that God's people may be up to the task ahead and have all they need to accomplish every good work"* (2 Timothy 3:16–17 The Voice).

VISION

In essence **Culture Changers** is an expression of the Family of God in operation on the earth today with love for both the world and the church. We meet as Family and, as followers of Jesus, we know we have a mandate to change our world, knowing we need to connect with others like ourselves as we do so.

In practical terms we have a passion to establish and connect Kingdom Families - His Families that will impact our local communities. These families will be safe places where all are loved and honoured; where we can grow and experience the Father Heart of God; where the Kingdom of God can flourish and people can be renewed in their thinking; allowing miracles, signs and wonders to become part of a normal way of life; where Heaven meets earth and the presence of God is central every time we gather in simplicity, power and love.[3]

VALUES

Values are what we build our lives on. They are things we hold dear, concepts and ideas that are fundamental to us. They influence our lives and often motivate our decision making as well as our actions. Our priorities and practices flow from the values we have. **Culture Changers** values are:

FAMILY – Where oneness, fatherhood, intimacy, sonship, honour and faithfulness are hallmarks. From this come our priorities of connectivity, relationship with one another and with Jesus, and mutual accountability. In practice this means a family where the individual is valued, where we connect regularly, forgiving and being forgiven, wanting excellence and not perfection, equipping one another for a Kingdom lifestyle with reality, integrity, humility, honesty, mercy, courage and maturity.

WORSHIP – John Wimber wrote: "Worship is the highest delight a human being can experience when they do what gives God the greatest pleasure." Our priority is desiring to bring God great pleasure as we creatively follow Him, and to be generous in every area of our lives. Practically speaking this means – demonstrating our love for Him by the way we live. To be a faithful and persevering people, regardless of our outward circumstances, and to grow in a lifestyle of worship, being recognised as ambassadors of hope and joy.

REVELATION – We value the Bible (both the *rhema* word from God to each individual or to a people today, and also God's written Word, *logos*, as we read it in the Bible). We equally value the Holy Spirit's revelation, empowering us to bring "Heaven to earth." Our priority is to be with God, enquiring of Him, relishing His overwhelming presence, being led by His presence and moving in signs and wonders. Coming from this place of stillness, intimacy and rest, in practice we become His ambassadors and atmosphere changers. **Culture Changers** bring hope, love and mercy to the world around them.

LOVE – We highly value His love and goodness which we want to undergird everything we stand for. Our priority is to encounter His love, to learn to love ourselves and also to love and honour one another – demonstrating this with love and joy! We believe we owe the world an encounter with our good God. Practically speaking, as defenders of the weak, this means we want to reach out with His love to the marginalised and disadvantaged, bringing love, mercy and justice wherever we go. It is our joy to remember that hell's trash is heaven's treasure![4]

WHAT HAPPENS WHEN WE CONNECT?

Being in God's family, our desire as **Culture Changers** is to spend time together. As intimacy grows, our longing to be in His presence increases. It is being connected that matters – connected with Him and with one another. Our priority is our relationship rather than our orthodoxy. In these times together, everyone enjoys the freedom of the Spirit and respects and honours each other, submitting to one another, being devoted to one another, wanting the best for one another, being generous to one another. In this non–competitive environment we can naturally be equipped, empowered and encouraged.

Whether sharing a meal, going for a walk, breaking bread, doing life together, being baptised as a new follower of Jesus, praying for one another, watching a film – these are times when believers just enjoy being together. In fact they become devoted rather than committed to one another. In connecting as a family there is no format because families don't have format!

Revelation from the Bible and the Holy Spirit are foundational to us. We are led by the Spirit in a corporate way as we listen to the present truth gleaned from the revelations of one another and from what we are hearing God say. This is natural, dynamic, loving and equally important, fun. As others observe the change in us – so they too may want to meet this Jesus (see Appendix One)!

In this "flat" network the subject of covering is vital. In 2013, the Lord gave us a supernatural sign to confirm that for us in **Culture Changers** our covering on earth can be access to wise, godly men and women with whom we have relationship. *Hebrews 8: 10b - 12 "I will put my laws in their minds and write them on their hearts. I will be their God and they will be my people. No longer will a man teach his neighbour, or a man his brother, saying "Know the Lord" because they will all know me, from the least to the greatest. For I will forgive their wickedness and will remember their sins no more".* We believe that part of the Lord "wanting His Family back" is for us to know He hears us all and that each one of us can hear Him personally and be valued as an equal member of His Family.

As far as our giving is concerned, we enjoy the gift of giving so that our villages, towns, cities and nations are the beneficiaries. Our vision is to learn to value one another more than our possessions. To begin to see our resources being released to ensure that there are no needy ones amongst us or in our communities.

THE FAMILY

In His Family, all of us take our places and those who are more mature encourage others. Our homes become places of prayer, open doors for our communities, places of training and equipping, places of healing, places of learning, places where creativity may flourish and last, but not least, power houses in our local communities. In this safe, family setting we all know we can take our part in changing a nation by being changed ourselves; men, women, and children, who have had the revelation that we are sons and daughters of the King. We can spontaneously "connect" or even create a family environment whether in homes, shops, prisons, hostels, half–way houses, theatres, stadiums, circuses, cathedrals and government buildings, businesses, universities, schools and hospitals. In fact, wherever we feel most at home. We demonstrate "Oneness", believing we are to be aligned to other believers collectively in an area. Our model for this is taken from Ephesians 1:1 *"To the saints in Ephesus – the faithful in Christ Jesus."* We are those who connect regularly for friendship, fun and food. We share together our testimonies as well as our hopes and failures in a loving, non–competitive environment.

Culture Changers resonate with John 15:5 – "The vine and the branches." We love all expressions of the Church that Jesus is building and honour those that are different from our own. We long to see a time where individual agendas are put aside and a local unity in the Spirit begins to be established. A unity that is **vertical** rather than horizontal where relationship with our Father, through Jesus, is our common bond rather than seeking agreement between denominations. So the Church in a city is "One" with Jesus as her Head, rather than having numerous expressions which are separated by theological differences.

EndNotes

1 See www.quaker.org.uk

2 *John Wimber —His Influence And Legacy*, by David Pytches

3 Much of this para written by Jeremy and Yvette Britton - www.openheaven.co.uk

4 Bob Johnson

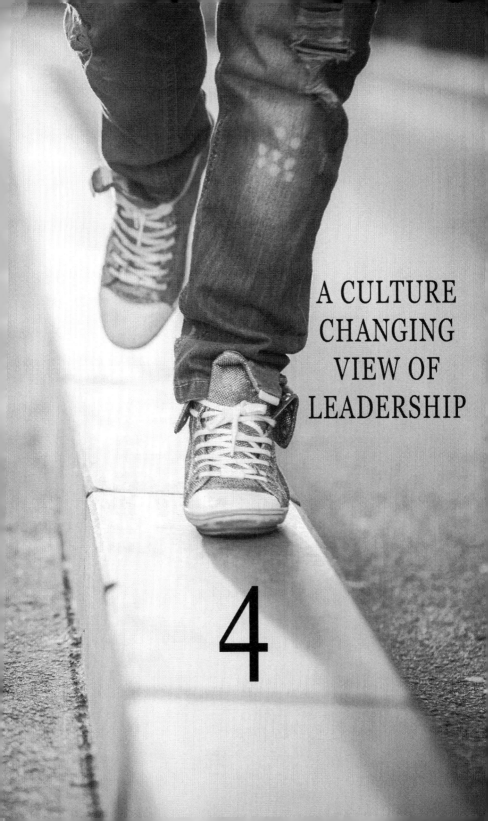

A CULTURE
CHANGING
VIEW OF
LEADERSHIP

4

Chapter Four

A CULTURE CHANGING VIEW OF LEADERSHIP

JESUS IS THE HEAD OF HIS CHURCH

Everyone agrees that Jesus is the Head of His Church - the book of Colossians 1:15-20 puts it in a nutshell! Colossians 1:15-20 NIV *"He is the image of the invisible God, the firstborn over all creation. For by him all things were created: things in heaven and on earth, visible and invisible, whether thrones or powers or rulers or authorities; all things were created by him and for him. He is before all things, and in him all things hold together. And he is the head of the body, the church; he is the beginning and the firstborn from among the dead, so that in everything he might have the supremacy. For God was pleased to have all his fullness dwell in him, [20] and through him to reconcile to himself all things, whether things on earth or things in heaven, by making peace through his blood, shed on the cross".* The Big Question is rather "How is this worked out in principle and practice!"

Speaking personally, I am reminded that Jesus is my Source – my starting point. He is the head of all creation and was there before the creation of the world (Genesis1:1-3 and John 1:1) and so He has made all things and knows all about them. He is the great initiator and sustains everything as 'He holds all things together'. He is the head of the church and there is no other! The scriptures confirm this by saying there is only one Chief Shepherd and it may be worth noting that even the Apostle Peter only dares call himself a 'fellow elder.'[1] The great challenge for us is to remember this daily as we walk with Him, enquire of Him and align ourselves to Him! (1 Corinthians 4:11-17).

THE TIME FOR 'POLICING' IS OVER

We believe a new breed of leaders is emerging – elders or spiritual parents formed in the hidden place who have a heart to serve rather than a need to control [2]. Leaders who are reminded that there is only One Pastor and that is The Good Shepherd.

Therefore, as **Culture Changers**, we see ourselves as a Family rather than a network or hierarchy – with a 'tribal' rather than a more 'organisational' style of leadership. The time for 'policing' is over. Make no mistake, we believe that godly leadership and recognition of authority are vital and constantly demonstrated in Scripture. Everyone has probably witnessed families where a young child can rule it by throwing tantrums until it gets its way. This is the result of the father and/ or mother not being what they are called to be. If there is a vacuum of leadership, you can count on the rebellious, the self-willed, or the self-promoting to fill it. This has destroyed many families, as well as many churches and organisations.[3]

It is the style of leadership that is in question. We believe that the Holy Spirit is releasing the apostolic gift to the Body of Christ and He defines that gift as spiritual parenting. This is made clear in 1 Corinthians 4:15 where Paul comments about how the Corinthians have many teachers but not many fathers, and in 1 Thessalonians 2:7 -12, where Paul teaches that the apostle is a spiritual Dad and / or Mum! He talks of a plural leadership of those naturally fulfilling the role of spiritual parents, emerging with an eagerness to see all God's children step out in their own spiritual gifts and grow into maturity. A family where those with a 'parenting' function provide a safe environment where others may flourish.

FREEDOM AND EMPOWERMENT

In this plural leadership, those with a father/mother heart would seek to support and be the foundation to all that God is calling others to. They delight in seeing their sons and daughters running on ahead of them. They encourage each of them to walk into their callings and destinies on the seven mountains of culture (See some testimonies from Chapter 5 "Reaching your Area of Influence"). This encouragement builds freedom and confidence, rather than leaving His children feeling inadvertently exploited as they take their part in building a monument to the "church leader's" ministry! In other words, we are moving from a model of policing and control to one characterised by freedom and empowerment. As a result emerging mums and dads, who have been born-again, empower those around them to thrive as carriers of His presence. This enables their spiritual children to pursue their God-given dream trusting the Scriptures and the Holy Spirit to lead them.

A PARENTAL MODEL OF APOSTLESHIP

This new breed of apostle, actually a recovery of the original, parental model of apostleship in the New Testament, is going to be part of God's transformation of church structure - from a hierarchical pyramid to a dynamic arrowhead (the pyramid tipped on its side)...

as the leaders at the base of the triangle serve, coach, release and cheer on God's people at the arrowhead.

As they advance together they are resolute that there is no other gospel than that 'Jesus gave himself for our sins to rescue us from this present evil age' Galatians 1:4. Jesus is their Saviour and their Head and they are aware that He has appointed His leaders on earth (whatever label they might, or might not, be given) and entrusts them with the privilege of caring and teaching His Family (Acts 20:28 and 1 Peter 5:2).

CELEBRATING OUR DIFFERENCES

Together they are free to rejoice in their own uniqueness and celebrate, rather than tolerate, their brothers and sisters – whether they be Jew or Gentile. This leadership style recognises the need for one another and knows that no one person has all the answers! Indeed as other followers of Jesus watch strong men and women submitting their views and thoughts and prayer responses to others, in trust and vulnerability, they see a powerful and attractive model to emulate. Rather than an autocracy, followers of Jesus see those they respect and love, come together to seek God's guidance about a certain matter knowing their own input has been added into the mix! These leaders are there to guide things, and to step in if things get out of hand or if someone is bringing in deception. They are not those with a need to dominate a gathering, but rather would encourage others to come forward as much as possible. They are those, of whatever age, who will be identified as having tender, prepared hearts. Those who have been through the fire and withstood the tests, those who know of God's faithfulness in the midst of joys, temptations, trials and betrayal. Most of all, they are those who are led by His Presence.

SUPERNATURAL BLUEPRINTS

In the Old Testament the Lord appoints individual key leaders such as Abraham, Joshua, David and Moses as a type of Christ. In the New Testament, however, God gives us His Son to lead us as our elder brother, and our Head. He is now the One who does the appointing of elders or spiritual parents. In the past, churches have, by and large, been led by pastor-teachers. In terms of the fivefold ministries, the Apostles, Prophets and Evangelists have been missing in leadership. We believe that this is about to change and that it is time for them to return. In particular it is time for the New Testament model of the apostles to emerge as fathers and mothers who bring supernatural blueprints from heaven. The emergence of this forgotten style of leadership will, therefore, be life transforming for His Family.

LEADERS WITH ONE ENTITLEMENT

This new breed of leaders know their identity as sons and daughters of the King. Leaders such as these will have had their orphan hearts healed and will be mature sons and daughters who have been raised up in a naturally supernatural flow to become fathers and mothers (who in turn empower mature sons and daughters). They have nothing to prove as they are honoured by their only entitlement - that they are children of God! They are His children and therefore princes and princesses in His Kingdom. They are free to be childlike leaders – although not childish! They know their authority as those who are seated with Him in heavenly places (Ephesians 2:6). From this perspective they have learnt to believe *like* Jesus and not just *in* Him! They live with an expectation of blessing as they advance the kingdom – courageously being on the offensive without fear of attack! They are those who have learnt to possess joy regardless of their current circumstances. They are those whose passion it is to empower, rather than control. Above all they are those who have learnt to lean into His Presence and let the government be on His shoulders and not theirs.

There is no 'one way' to formally recognise these leaders –rather just as cream rises to the top, so will they, and they will recognise that the rest of the milk is creamy too! The qualities Paul describes for elders and deacons are those which the work of the Holy Spirit brings about in every one of us. Therefore one of the primary joys of these elders is to identify others like them and to bless, encourage and equip these men and women in order that they too may become godly leaders for others to follow.

MEN *AND* WOMEN PREPARE THE BRIDE

The prophet Joel (Joel 2:28-32) says that in the last days the Lord will pour out His Spirit on both men and women. Indeed, many of the principal leaders in the ever expanding Chinese Church are women[4]. In these days when the Bride is being prepared, it is no surprise She is also attended by women – it would be an odd bride that wanted only male attendants! In these last days it is who we are in Christ that matters! As One New Man there is no Jew or Gentile, male or female etc. – although we are to honour one another and our unique differences. It is amusing to remember that women are included as 'Sons of God' and men are included in the 'Bride of Christ'.

These Fathers and Mothers will be recognised as having the ability to teach, to protect, to take responsibility, to give wisdom and to settle disagreements for those in their care. This is their privilege – just as is their desire to make sure that any sick or needy ones amongst them are looked after. This, in turn, builds an atmosphere of trust and safety, and earns them the respect they deserve (1 Timothy, Titus, and I Peter 5:2-3). They are amazing because HE is amazing!

EVERYONE NEEDS ACCOUNTABILITY

We all need accountability. Just as we follow the commandments of Jesus so we are to be accountable to others in whom we recognise the empowering of the Holy Spirit. As part of being devoted, rather than just committed to one another, we have a responsibility to honour and stand with those leaders to whom we have given permission to speak into our lives. These Fathers and Mothers will themselves be accountable and from time to time may need support. Some Streams would call this group of supporting leaders 'Overseers'[1]. Overseers are perhaps more experienced and mature Fathers and Mothers to whom others can turn. Overseers may sometimes be part of "The Five Fold Ministry.

THE FIVE FOLD MINISTRY

Leadership in the Father's Family is relational and, as explained earlier, parental. Complementary to their brothers and sisters there will be those who might be called The Five Fold Ministry. They will be those who can see and activate heaven's blueprints; those who can hear and see what the Lord is doing more clearly than others; those who have a gift of sharing their faith and building up the saints; those with a recognised gift of teaching and those who have a love for the whole church as pastors / shepherds. These men and women will not be in competition with one another but rather will complement one another as together they further equip His Family. For the purpose of this chapter, they will be those whom the elders, in other words the fathers and mothers, can turn to when they need further leadership support and expertise.

These are the men and woman who supply in us those things that are lacking – bringing us His life and refreshing in the process (1 Corinthians 16:15-18). Indeed we will want to imitate them and learn from them as they demonstrate godly wisdom, discernment and generosity. We will stand with them, and they with us. Should they be falsely accused we will stand together. This is a new season. With this model of humility and relationship, it will be the delight of these God ordained men and women, to facilitate maturity and equip His Family.

A SECOND REFORMATION?

In the process, we trust that the church will experience a second Reformation. In the first, Luther's theology was that "God is judge, we are lawbreakers, but the Cross secures our justification". This is a legal model. In the coming church, God will be seen as Dad, we will be seen as orphans who need saving, and the Cross will be understood as the price paid for our adoption. This is a family model and we love it! The belief that God is our Abba will turn the church from an institution or denomination into a family where fathers and mothers release sons and daughters to serve in their spheres of influence, where they are fulfilled in the revelation of His glory in them[5].

Theology always affects ecclesiology and ecclesiology always affects missiology[6]. These apostles, prophets, evangelists, teachers and shepherds will rejoice at the unique gifting of those with whom they are in relationship and it is their delight to help them mature. The power of the Lord will be upon them as they aspire to Jesus's model of sound leadership that can't be perverted or shaken. No more will these labels be a status symbol - but rather a function, as the emerging Five Fold will happily submit to one another whilst equipping His Family together – as one – on earth as it is in heaven.

EndNotes

1 Bob Deffinbaugh "The New Testament Church – Its leadership".

2 *See Appendix Three for Bob Jones' Prophecy http:// www.propheticdestinyministries.org/2011/02/25/ isaiah–2222–key–of–david– company/*

3 Attribute to Rick Joyner "True Leadership" Week 45 (2014) from the Great Commission

4 Paul Golf – The Coming Chinese Church

5 Psalm 17:15b The Passion Translation

6 Mark Stibbe

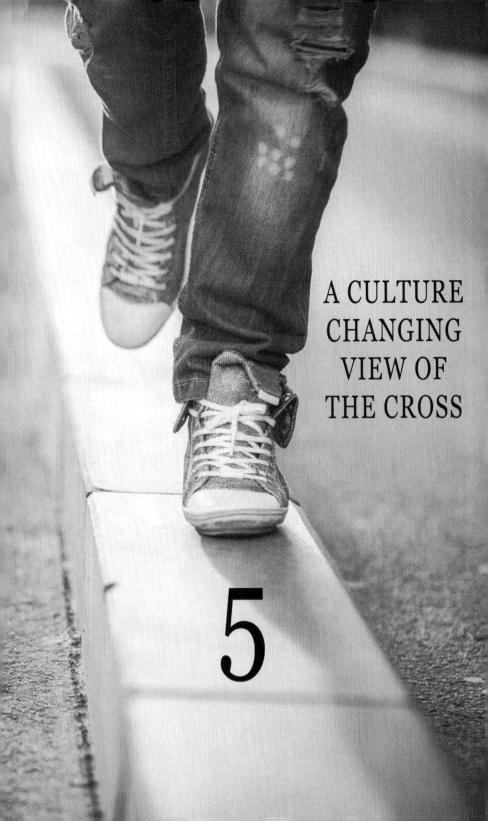

A CULTURE
CHANGING
VIEW OF
THE CROSS

5

Chapter Five

A CULTURE CHANGING VIEW OF THE CROSS

Mark Stibbe

I am so grateful to Hugh and Ginny for the opportunity to share a few thoughts about the Cross. During my season of brokenness, I have spent a lot of time at Calvary, meditating on the depths of Christ's suffering, seeking to understand more about what the Passion really means to us. This has led me to formalize and crystallize my thoughts in a book called *My Father's Tears*, subtitled, 'The Cross and the Father's Love.'

REDISCOVERING SPIRITUAL ADOPTION

My time of meditation and research into what we have historically taught about the Cross has led me to believe that what we have so often understood by the word 'atonement' is not wrong. It's just not complete enough. Traditionally we have focused our views around ideas from the law court (justification), the slave market (redemption), the battlefield (Christ the Victor), the Temple (substitution/satisfaction) and the political arena (reconciliation). None of this I would want to jettison but there's another picture in the Bible - an idea taken from the home and the family, which focuses on adoption. What if we were to explore this far more family-based understanding of the Cross?

For many years now I have been writing about the extraordinary but much neglected idea of spiritual adoption. As I've pointed out in books like *From Orphans to Heirs*, it was principally the Apostle Paul who exploited this rich metaphor of salvation. He was basing his thoughts on the Roman practice of adoption, in which a young male slave would be bought out of their servitude by a man who longed for a son. This process of adoption involved two stages:

STAGE 1: THE TRANSACTION

The adopting father would go to a magistrate with the slave child and his natural father. Three times the biological father would sell the boy to the adopting father for an agreed price. This would be conducted before the praetor or magistrate and in the presence of seven witnesses. These witnesses would be able to testify for the rest of the boy's life that he was indeed the adopting father's son.

STAGE 2: THE DECLARATION

After the third sale, the magistrate would declare that the boy was the adopting father's son and heir. He was from that moment on released from the fatherly authority of the natural father and placed under the fatherly authority of the adopting father. All the boy's previous debts would be cancelled and the boy from that moment on would have a new father, a new family, a new future, a new fortune and above all a new freedom.

ADOPTION AND THE CROSS

The Apostle Paul, by background a Roman citizen as well as a devout Jew, looked at this Roman rite of adoption and under the leading of the Holy Spirit saw it as a magnificent metaphor for both Israel's adoption as a nation and the believer's adoption too.

As far as Israel was concerned, Paul saw with eyes enlightened by the Holy Spirit that God the Father had chosen Israel out of every nation under the sun and decided to grant it the special privilege of standing in the same position before him as a firstborn son. This is why through Moses (an adopted child, please note) God rescued Israel from slavery under Pharaoh. It is why Paul says of the Jewish people 'theirs is the adoption as sons' (Romans 9:4).

But there's more!

Paul went on to apply this metaphor to those who are 'in Christ.' Believers are delivered from spiritual slavery (both slavery to the Law and slavery to sin) and given an undeserved freedom. This freedom was not paid for by silver or gold but by the precious blood of Christ. Jesus, the only Son of God by *nature,* paid the price and as a result of his amazing sacrifice we are adopted into a new family. As I wrote way back in *From Orphans to Heirs,* we are therefore no longer under the authority of the father of lies but under the authority of the Father of Lights. All our previous debts have been cancelled. We can now call God Abba Father and rejoice in the fact that the Spirit (like the seven witnesses in the ancient Roman courts) testifies to our spirits that we truly are the children of God (Romans 8:15-16).

A RICHER VIEW OF THE ATONEMENT

All this leads to a much more familial view of the Cross. The other major views of the atonement (justification, redemption, Christus Victor, substitution and reconciliation) are relational. But this view, focused on adoption, is the most relational of all. In fact it is familial - based around family and home.

As we look at this new model of the atonement in greater depth, we begin to gain some insights that are by and large lost or undervalued in the other views of the atonement. Take for example the role of Israel.

In the adoption view of the Cross, the long history of Israel's adoption by the Father becomes the meta-narrative or big story in which our adoption in Christ is truly understood and honoured. What has happened to Israel nationally has happened to us individually. Ethnic adoption has now been developed into personal adoption, but all within the context of the family of the Jewish people, whom the Father still loves, for in his eyes, 'once adopted, always adopted.'

Then take the Trinity. In most views of the atonement, the inter-relationships between the three persons of God are often neglected when we talk about the Cross. But in this model, we begin to experience the indescribable agony of the Father watching his Son's passion. We see the Son in his fully human heart experiencing the devastating plight of the orphan - which is separation from a father - and embracing this sense of abandonment for our sakes. And finally we capture a glimpse of the Holy Spirit, the bond of eternal love within the Trinity, holding the Father and the Son in an eternal embrace in heaven even while the drama of abandonment is being felt by both as the passion continues on its grisly and inexorable path here on earth.

For these two gains alone, I would say let's give much more attention to an adoption-shaped view of the Calvary event.

AN END TO THE ORPHAN CONDITION

Seen in this light, the promise made by Jesus to the disciples the night before he died takes on a new and luminous significance. In John 14:18 he tells them, 'I will not leave you as orphans.' The word 'orphan' within the Bible means someone who has lost their father (*orphanos* in the New Testament, *yattam* in the Old). Jesus is clearly not speaking literally here because these men whom he is addressing have fathers. He is speaking figuratively, reassuring them that the state that all human beings have endured since the Fall - which can be summed up as 'the orphan condition', by which is meant separation (because of sin) from *Abba* Father - is about to be radically addressed through Christ's self-giving sacrifice at the Cross, a sacrifice in which he will pay the price by which they and all others who follow in their footsteps can transition from slavery into sonship. He is promising, 'no more orphans!'

All this sheds a piercing and comforting light on the darkness of Golgotha. Here, in effect, Jesus embraces in his fully human heart the agony of our orphan condition since the Fall. For our sakes he endures the consciousness of his precious Abba's absence. He cries, 'my God, my God, why have you abandoned me?' Put another way, the Son becomes a spiritual orphan so that we who are spiritual orphans might become sons and daughters.

What a Son!
What a Saviour!
What an older Brother!

THE GOSPEL FOR A FATHERLESS GENERATION

I have a conviction that in this fatherless world, this picture of the Father weeping over his Son, and the Son embracing the fullness of the orphan condition at Calvary, is truly 'Gospel'. It is, in other words, Good News. People all over the world are desperate to hear that there is a Dad in heaven who loves them like no earthly father ever could, a Dad who longs to adopt them into his family and become for them the father they've been waiting for all their lives.

What if we were to use this neglected Biblical and family-based picture, this idea of adoption, in our sensitive communication of the Gospel?

My experience is that the lights come on in people's eyes when I share this message. In fact, often their eyes start to mist and then fill.

In response to the Father's tears, their tears begin to fall as well.

I started this by saying 'I believe.' I'm going to finish it the same way. I believe that this adoption-based understanding of the Cross is the premier way for us to share the Good News in this orphan generation. I'm not saying that we should lay aside the other models of the atonement. I'm saying that we need to take this forgotten jewel from the treasure trove of Scripture, brush it down, clean it up, and present it with humble and caring hands to hairdressers, postmen, teachers and firemen - to the young and the old and to the poor and the rich.

We need to tell them what Jesus told the lost daughter of Samaria (paraphrasing), 'there's a Daddy in heaven that's crazy about you. And I'm here to tell you about him, demonstrate his extreme love, and hug the hell out of you.' When she heard that, the effect was electric. When our generation hears and sees it, the effect will be the same.

RAINDROPS KEEP FALLING

In Mel Gibson's film *The Passion of the Christ*, there is a moment of tenderness in the midst of what is otherwise unremitting and intense brutality. As Jesus dies on the Cross, a raindrop falls from the sky and lands at the foot of the Cross as the Son breathes his last breath. The raindrop is an unforgettable symbol for the Father's tears.

These tears are still falling, especially for this fatherless world where countless millions of people not only lack an earthly father but also a saving and intimate knowledge of their loving *Abba* in heaven.

Raindrops truly keep on falling.

So let's rediscover the glorious truth of our adoption in Christ. Let's do in our generation with the doctrine of adoption what Luther did with the doctrine of justification in his. In other words, let's position ourselves for a new Reformation. When we do, it will not only change church culture. It will change the cultures of the world too.

Mark Stibbe's book, *My Father's Tears. The Cross and the Father's Love* is published by SPCK. This chapter is Mark's summary, written especially for this book.

A NEW
ERA

6

Chapter Six

A NEW ERA

HEAVEN'S AMBASSADORS ON EARTH

We believe in Heaven and we believe in hell[1] – forgiveness being the key to our new destination. Yet being forgiven is just the start, not the end of our journey. The good news is that we can live beyond the cross and, yes, even beyond Pentecost. As we become part of God's family – born again by the power of the Holy Spirit – we learn to see things from a Heavenly perspective. From this advantageous position, growing to know our Heavenly Father more and more each day, we are equipped to be His ambassadors in this world and our homes become embassies for His Kingdom on earth. Our assignment is "to do what we see the Father doing", partnering with Him to bring His Kingdom to earth

Writing from his prison cell, probably in Rome, the

Apostle Paul describes all liberated believers as occupying a new spiritual location – we are now "seated with Jesus in the Heavenly realms." In this place, we enjoy all the spiritual blessings God has prearranged for us, but we also wait for the next act in the drama of redemption. We have already been raised to live in this new reality, but the world is still not what it will be when the Anointed One, the liberating King, comes again. Even now, Jesus is positioned at God's right hand reigning over the spiritual powers that many of us have feared most. Paul assures us that, as we belong to Jesus and take up the full armour of God, we have nothing to fear.[2]

As Bill Johnson puts it: "We realise that before God we are an Intimate, before people we are servants, and before the powers of hell, we are rulers, with no tolerance of their influence."

SHIFTING FROM THE KNOWN TO THE UNKNOWN

George Barna says: "Shifting from the known to the unknown is always uncomfortable, but intelligent and responsive changes will birth a church better able to minister effectively in the new Millennium." Whatever church currently looks like for us – it will take courage to move forward. A core value for us is to get back to child–like simplicity, encouraging and spurring one another on to make a difference in the world around us.

Our foundational call is to be positioned and to live as ambassadors of the Kingdom, seeking to re–align ourselves, our thinking, behaviours, lifestyle and culture, to this new season. We live in one culture but we are called to establish another – the culture of Heaven! In this way, we become part of the response to Jesus' prayer "Your Kingdom come on earth as it is in Heaven." Equally, as we share His love with the world around us we also take our part in fulfilling the words of Habakkuk 2:14, *"For the earth will be filled with the knowledge of the glory of the LORD, as the waters cover the sea."*

I recently read the following in relation to the early church: "Although this young and thriving church has no political influence, property, fame or wealth – it is powerful. Its power is centred in living the gospel. The people value one another more than any possessions. They come together as a large, passionate, healthy family where it is natural to pray and share all of life together. The Kingdom of God is blossoming on earth as these lovers of God embrace the teachings of Jesus."[3]

FURTHER EQUIPPING FOR THIS SEASON

To help us further embrace this new season, Hugh and I have been greatly blessed by Paul Manwaring's input into our lives. His ministry, "Global Legacy", is a relational network that connects, encourages, and equips revival leaders worldwide. They expand God's Kingdom by helping to build relationships between revival leaders, ministries and organisations around the globe, and to equip them to transform their spheres of influence. Paul writes that we cannot change the culture (shared knowledge, beliefs and behaviours) around us without first changing the culture **within** us. We believe that these cultures have been instrumental in changing our earthly viewpoint to be more aligned with His Heavenly perspective. Here are some of the cultures that we have found life transforming[4]:

1. **The Goodness of God** – "To experience God's goodness in such a powerful way that it profoundly and positively impacts our life and ministry."

2. **Salvation** – "To increase passion and effectiveness to personally and corporately influence many to become born again disciples of Jesus Christ."

3. **Joy and Hope** – "To live lives that are infused with joy and hope."

4. **Faith and Risk** –"Leaders setting the standard by pushing the envelope of their comfort zones because of a revelation of the size of God within them."

5. **Grace and Empowerment** – "Grace is active power – Harold Eberle. To experience grace in ourselves in order to empower grace in others."

6. **Valuing His Presence** – "That each of us will personally and corporately increase our experience

and value for His presence – there is nothing more precious."

7. **Honour** – "Honour releases life. Releasing life by recognising the Glory that is on one another."

8. **Releasing the Supernatural** – "Living beyond what we can do."

9. **The Prophetic** – "Calling out the gold in people. To live a prophetic lifestyle in order to lead a prophetic culture."

10. **Generosity** – "Give and it will be given to you. Building a lifestyle of generosity that changes lives, impacts cities and brings revival."

11. **Family Culture** – "Learning to value heart connections in relationships which help to identify where you might be in your relationship with your Heavenly Father: – Elder Brother (orphan spirit, performance attitude, self-hatred and critical spirit); or A Son at Home (rest, favour, heart connections)"

12. **Revelation and the Word Culture** – "Emphasizing the importance of abiding in the Word in order that the truth that you know can set you free (John 8:31-32). Valuing conversations that overflow with Scripture, teaching and the prophetic ministry (Jeremiah 20:9) and interpreting Scripture through the finished work of the cross (2 Corinthians 3:6)

THE NEW ERA

As more and more people search for spiritual significance and start experiencing intimacy with their Heavenly Father, they will begin to see themselves as children of the King. They will grow in understanding that, as such, they too have the ability to change the world around them with the love of God they carry. Journeying with God more fully into this new season brings challenges to our mind-sets and comfort zones. This means: gladly embracing accelerated change; willingly allowing the Holy Spirit to renew our minds (especially when it collides with our theology!); being unreservedly vulnerable to the "light" of the Holy Spirit flooding our beings; responding to God for yet deeper levels of intimacy with our Abba, Jesus and Holy Spirit and – last but not least - realising we may be the "culmination generation" and learning to think and live from that revelation.[5] With this in mind, I hope the following insights may help us all to live a transformed life through a scriptural renewing of our minds. These observations will hopefully describe part of the spiritual **shift** that appears to be happening amongst many of God's people at the moment.

SONSHIP

In this new season the church is rising up to take her place as sons and daughters of the King including recognizing their heavenly ethnicity. In the old season many of us were unaware that once we are born again we become part of God's royal family. We lived therefore with "orphan and victim–like" tendencies. Many were uncertain of their identity and therefore tried to earn God's favour and blessings. Yet the church is now learning that we are greatly loved, we have been adopted into the Father's family and we have the full inheritance as His sons and daughters. We are, therefore, not only adopted into our Heavenly Father's family but we become spiritual princes, princesses, kings and queens – in His Kingdom! He is the King of Kings and, as His kids, we naturally have royal titles too. Seated with him in Heavenly places (Ephesians 2:6), we walk in His royal authority. We walk in larger faith – knowing that we are spirit beings and not just "mere" men (1 Corinthians 3:3).

Wendy Backlund[6] puts it so well when she writes, "We are first and foremost a spirit living in a natural body as we learn to see, hear and access the spirit realm and its principles." (*2 Corinthians 5:16 "So from now on we regard no one from a worldly point of view. Though we once regarded Christ in this way, we do so no longer. Therefore, if anyone is in Christ, he is a new creation; the old has gone and the new has come!"*)

Her book *"Living from the Unseen"* reveals that we can live life through the eyes of the spirit with an awareness of the spiritual realities and principles that affect our everyday lives. Believing differently, not trying harder, is the key to change.

HEAVEN'S RELATIONAL GOVERNMENT

In this new season, the church is recognising the joy of relationship over organisation. As we see Father, Jesus and Holy Spirit relate together – so we are given their model to follow. The various facets of Jesus are represented on earth through the gifts to us all of apostles, prophets, evangelists, teachers and shepherds. Known as the Five Fold Ministers, these equippers of the family are learning to serve together and serve one another. Whilst they all seek the Kingdom of God, the apostles and the prophets enquire and activate blueprints from Heaven, and the teachers, evangelists and shepherds help to interpret these revelations to God's family. So we are all equipped in the supernatural and released to change the world around us.

BRIDE AND INTIMACY

Although Jesus talks of us as his family and friends, the depth of intimacy to which he calls us is reflected in the language used in the book of Revelation, which tells us that he is returning for a "Bride." As His Family is reconnected, so together we become His Bride – and have an ever-deepening relationship with Him. It may be worth noting that the oil in the five virgins' lamps was the oil that came from their closeness to Jesus rather than their performance. He is jealous for us! Now may be the time to put our own lives through a filter, knowing that one day we will stand before God on our own. Somehow that gives me an urgency to deal with my own "spots and blemishes". In this season, the kindness of God seems to be asking many of us if we are personally prepared for His coming.

VALUING EVERYONE'S INPUT

While we want to know him individually, it is when we come together that God distributes His gifts to us all. So it is not just the meeting together that is important – rather the gathering in a setting where there is space for everyone to contribute. Without one another we are incomplete.

OUR HOMES – HIS EMBASSIES

In this new era our homes can become embassies for Jesus our King. Embassies where His relational government, His ways, His blueprints and His inventions will become the way and the means by which Heaven will bless the earth.

In these embassies we recognise we are citizens of Heaven,first. For those of us who are married – our marriages are unique windows made available to those around us to closely watch and observe our loving relationships as husbands and wives (Ephesians 5:22-30). As a happy marriage is a prophetic reflection of the Kingdom theme of Jesus marrying His bride, so the natural response of the children and other members of the household is to want to give their parents both respect and obedience. (1 Tim 3:1-13,Titus 1:6-11)[7]

These embassies can equally be made up of a few young people deciding to share life based on Kingdom principles. Alternatively, a senior citizen in a sad, empty house can open it up to be filled with life again! It typically begins where people, in the name of Jesus Christ, open their houses, their kitchens, their fridges, and share in the common wealth of the Kingdom in very practical ways right where they live. Places where everyone has something to contribute and receive – as they follow Jesus together – knowing He is their King, their brother, their law giver and, not least, their economic director.[7]

PRESENCE AND RELATIONSHIP

The presence of The Lord is our treasure. It is Him that we seek and with Him we want to stay. Resting in His presence, we become increasingly sensitive to His heart and His voice. He shows us where to go and what to do. Our wisdom, along with Moses and Barak, is to say "Don't send me out unless you go with me." The presence of the Lord is the signal that miracles are about to take place and prisoners set free. However, it is enough to know that He is with us – or should I say "they" are with us – the Father, Jesus and Holy Spirit. No one can compare with them or offer the unconditional love that they do.

In this new era, connectivity will increasingly become a very high value and the Holy Spirit will take centre stage. The season for leaders using control to disciple people is coming to an end. Instead, as the saints, we will be encouraged to hear the voice of the Lord for ourselves and our walk with God will flow out of our connection with the Holy Spirit. *"This is the covenant I will make with the people of Israel after that time" declares the Lord. "I will put my law in their minds and write it on their hearts. I will be their God, and they will be my people. No longer will they teach their neighbour or say to one another 'Know the Lord' because they will know me, from the least of them to the greatest," declares the Lord. "For I will forgive their wickedness and will remember their sins no more." (Jeremiah 31:33-35)*

PRAY FOR THE PEACE OF JERUSALEM

Isaiah 62:2 (The Voice Translation) says "Jerusalem, the nations of the world will witness your righteousness, the most powerful world leaders will see your brilliance". We believe that although we may not know the hour or the day of the return of Jesus, we are to be ready to discern the season. When He comes back He will have leadership over all the earth and Jerusalem will be His headquarters. Just as the land of Israel is the Lord's, so is Jerusalem His capital. What is more, He will come as King – and His coming Church will be walking in the path of His commandments – not considering them just suggestions.

In loving obedience to Psalm 122:6, we are to pray for the fulfilling of God's plan for Jerusalem to be His House for His people – both Jew and Gentile – where Jesus will rule as the Prince of Peace. In the meantime, our prayers can include interceding for His purposes to be fulfilled there, for Jerusalem to remain under Jewish sovereignty and for special protection for the City and its inhabitants (Psalm 122:8).

LIFESTYLE OF WORSHIP

In this new day our worship is not limited to singing praises to God during set corporate times. As Psalm 101:2 implies – we seek to lead lives of integrity. As we behold Him, as we abide, rest, soak in His presence, worship flows out from us and we establish a lifestyle of praise, worship and thanksgiving, ushering in Heaven's atmosphere wherever we are. As we remain in Him and He remains in us, so we worship Him in Spirit and in Truth, beholding Him and reading His Word.

FREEDOM AND EMPOWERMENT

We are in a season when we love to see the Holy Spirit take control of all we do. Within the safety of a family setting we can grow in confidence, freedom and empowerment as we step into our individual destinies. One of our highest priorities is to be non–hierarchical where everyone gets to play and our strengths are added to those around us.

ENCOUNTERS

Recognising and walking in His presence is the encounter we seek. We wait and watch for his presence and enjoy "staying with Him" as much as "going with Him." As we enter this new season, we want people to meet a liberating Jesus and not a controlling church!

Atmospheres change when we put the power of God's love before His truth. If people encounter God's love when they meet us – we may then have the opportunity of sharing His truth with them. However, if we just want them to know His truth – we may never get the opportunity to share His love. Just one touch from the King changes everything.

EXPECTATION OF BLESSING

As part of the renewal of our minds, and as we see things from a Heavenly perspective, we come to realise the true inheritance that we have. Therefore we live in a fresh reality of seeing the glass half full, rather than half empty. We speak and bring life with an expectation of God's intervention and blessing rather than viewing things from a standpoint of desperation. This is the difference between the orphan view and the view from being seated in Heavenly places as a son or a daughter.

REST

In this new season rest becomes part of our lives. We are realising that rest isn't inactivity; it is trusting God for the day rather than providing for ourselves by our own efforts. What is more, we now notice that frequently we seem to have a fuller release of blessings and revelations when we honour one day off a week in this way.

REVELATION

From a place of resting in His Presence, we learn to walk with the Lord and receive the revelation and impartation that He longs to give us, day by day. In this way we receive directly from Him and grow in knowing Him intimately. We are called to walk as friends of God, knowing Him beyond academic knowledge. To truly know someone you have to experience them.

AUTHORITATIVE
DECLARATIONS and PRAYER

Prayers that plead with God often come from an orphan mindset, failing to grasp the incredible authority that we have been given. In this new era, when we encounter problems, we won't just talk about them; we will speak into the situation, exercising our authority as sons and daughters of God. We are to declare what we hear the Lord saying to us. Our words can bring difficult situations into alignment with God's Kingdom, manifesting His goodness everywhere we go. We are to declare hope, encouragement and life over ourselves and others – knowing our words carry power. Steve Backlund's book *Igniting Faith* was a real eye–opener as we became aware of how much negativity came out of our mouths on a daily basis! In Steve's book we learnt to change our way of thinking and speaking as we started a negativity fast![8]

In Proverbs 18:21 we are reminded that "the tongue has the power of life and death." As we dismantle the lies of the enemy that we have believed and allowed to influence us, we are built up by what God says about us instead. In doing so we are deciding to choose "life" not "death" – replacing the enemy's lies with God's truth. (See Appendix Two for *Healing Declarations* and also www.liebusters.org).

Additionally, as citizens of another Kingdom, we have all been given another language. Speaking in tongues is the language of the Spirit and has great power in our daily lives. The apostle Paul urges us to use this gift – not just to express our love for God but also when we need renewed strength, revelation or wisdom.

OFFENSIVE MINDSET

We are moving from a defensive to an offensive mindset. We are called to "conquer" rather than "cope" or "cower." The children of Israel had to go from a "survival" mentality to a "conquering army" approach in a few days! God was in both scenarios, but only those who had an offensive mindset and did not shrink back were able to enter their destiny. In the past, many of us have been taught to take a defensive, rather than an offensive, stance against the enemy. Part of the renewing of our minds is to get satan's intimidating ways out of our brains as fast as possible. Jesus is our model. He interacted with the devil in the desert, in a brief encounter after which He sent him packing. Bob Goff puts it so well, "Jesus had a relationship with God that satan didn't understand. Jesus had no problem in telling him off and then getting rid of him. I think we should do the same. That's all I have to say about satan. He gets too much airtime already."

With our family around us, we wait for our Dad's instructions in the heat of battle – knowing He will back us up as His presence is with us.

JOYFUL

Everyone loves being around a joyful person – and Jesus was more joyful than all his companions (Hebrews 1:9). Sometimes joy comes naturally, but there are times when joy is a decision! We don't need to wait for circumstances to change before deciding to rejoice – in fact our rejoicing will change our circumstances! This joy reflects a Heavenly reality that is above any earthly circumstances. Steve Backlund's book *Possessing Joy* is very helpful in this regard.[9]

CREATING CHANGE

As change is a constant – we might as well learn to love it! There is a flow and an ease when we are synchronised with what God is doing even if we may be swimming against the earthly current. It is our role to discern what He is doing and then do as He does. If you are a visionary be aware that it isn't that everyone else is slow – it is just that you can see further down the road than them.

THE COMMON WEALTH OF GOD!

In the Kingdom of God we believe the time is coming when the mammon-driven economy will be replaced by the most fascinating, liberating and God-honouring economy this world will ever see: the Commonwealth of God. From the safety of these embassies God is calling those who have ears to hear to become part of a prophetic people, returning back to His economy as He gives them Heavenly blueprints for the good of the earth. As we learn to pray "Your Kingdom Come and my kingdom go!" so we have the privilege of participating in making His business, not ours, successful.[7]

FEAR OF THE LORD

As we are seated with Jesus in heavenly places, we are enabled to recognise that the battle we fight is not an equal battle. The question has to be asked "Just how big is my God?" His people are those who believe and stand on the truth that nothing is impossible for our amazing, awesome Abba Father! The counter balance to this is that we are reminded that the fear of the Lord is the beginning of wisdom.

Friendship with God does not carry with it a 'carte blanche' familiarity. Our comparisons of human friendship in relation to God can only go so far, because human friendship denotes friendship between two equals. With God, this is decidedly not the case. Few in the Old Testament understood God's heart as David did, but even he was struck with reverence and fear when he realized the greatness and holiness he was dealing with. God is not a human, and we treat Him as such at our own peril - there is a reason why we don't call our earthly fathers by their first names. Similarly a balance between a familiar friendship and holy respect must be struck when communicating with the God of the Universe. He may be my "Abba Daddy" but I need to bear in mind He is not my buddy![10]

FORCEFUL AND COURAGEOUS

In this new season, the church is being called to move from a spirit of fear and timidity to one of courage and forcefulness as Ezra 4:4 implies when, no matter their fear, God's people continued to be obedient. Our current culture finds it difficult to comprehend that God might deliberately endanger someone's life. We must remember that when God puts your life in danger, you are elevated into an elite group that is so precious that He never takes His eyes off you.[11]

SUPERNATURAL

The coming church continues to be released into a world of supernatural expectation and experience based upon Her reliance on the Word of God and the Holy Spirit. We will be equipped with both the presence and the presents of God.[12] We are recovering our rightful place as a supernatural people. Being born-again is non negotiable. We, as sons and daughters of our Warrior King, wage a supernatural fight with weapons that have divine power to demolish strongholds. We are taught supernaturally as we abide in our Abba Daddy, Jesus and the Holy Spirit and recognize that nothing is impossible for Them.

A FIGHT TO THE FINISH

As we step out of the box – resting and trusting, however scared we may be – we discover that there is no other way to live! Our focus is on our Dad, Jesus and the Holy Spirit, yet we are unwise to ignore the devil's schemes. As we follow the Great Commission and reach out to the sick, the oppressed and the prisoners, we are reminded that our names are written in the Book of Life and we have full authority over the enemy. The following quote from Ephesians 6:10–13 (The Message) puts it this way:

"And that about wraps it up. God is strong, and

he wants you strong. So take everything the Master has set out for you, well–made weapons of the best materials. And put them to use so you will be able to stand up to everything the Devil throws your way.

This is no afternoon athletic contest that we'll walk away from and forget about in a couple of hours. This is for keeps, a life–or–death fight to the finish against the Devil and all his angels. Be prepared. You're up against far more than you can handle on your own. Take all the help you can get, every weapon God has issued, so that when it's all over but the shouting, you'll still be on your feet. Truth, righteousness, peace, faith, and salvation are more than words. Learn how to apply them. You'll need them throughout your life. God's Word is an indispensable weapon. In the same way, prayer is essential in this ongoing warfare. Pray hard and long. Pray for your brothers and sisters. Keep your eyes open. Keep each other's spirits up so that no one falls behind or drops out."

EndNotes

1 Hell or Heaven in the Last Days – John Wright – www.branchpress.com

2 Introduction to the Book of Ephesians in the Voice Translation

3 Acts 2 in the Voice Translation

4 Paul Manwaring, www.igloballegacy.org

5 Jonathan Bugden

6 Wendy Backlund, Living From The Unseen

7 Wolfgang Simson – "The Kingdom Manifesto"

8 Steve Backlund – "Igniting Faith".

9 Steve Backlund – "Possessing Joy".

10 Darren Wilson "Finding God in the Bible"

11 Quote from Mario Murillo

12 Mark Stibbe "The Presents of God"

REACHING
YOUR
AREA OF
INFLUENCE

7

Chapter Seven

REACHING YOUR AREA OF INFLUENCE

As ambassadors for the Kingdom of God, we are all created to be contributors to society. To help us identify our areas of influence, Lance Wallnau has helpfully divided them into seven categories which he calls "the seven mountains": Economy, Government, Arts and Media, Education, Science and Technology, Family and Faith. Every person has the ability to influence one or more of these spheres through their actions and prayers. God sends His people to impact all these mountains with Kingdom culture and values and to share His message that He didn't come to condemn the world but to save it (John 3:17). The unpalatable truth is that just as Heaven is a reality – so is hell. It is our responsibility and, indeed, our joy to share what Jesus has done for us and see His standard raised once again in our nations.

God's love changes the world inside us, which in turn

changes the world around us. It is a joy to see in the following testimonies how some of us are seeing change in one or even a number of our areas of influence.

ARTS AND MEDIA

Our creations, stories, ideas, music and games and the way we communicate them. Entertainment, the press, sports, novels, myths, the internet, television, music, etc.

Helena Cavan, a poet and composer, writes: "Be a content provider!" This call came to me two years ago when I was preparing to speak at a seminar for Christians working in the Creative Arts. I felt Him underlining powerfully that He is calling for content! As **Culture Changers**, I believe He wants us to be filling the planet with holy content that glorifies Him as Creator of Heaven and earth. Why? Because when we are most ourselves, walking our destiny–path, He is most glorified! Sir Ken Robinson talks and writes about people being "in their element." When we are "in our element", we most glorify God because we radiate with joy, purpose, passion, fulfillment and contentment. We are fully resourced and our resource–full state is highly attractive and magnetic.

Several years ago, I remember God very clearly saying, "Helena, I'm giving you the mantle of Emily Dickinson." I was shocked. I like Emily a lot! I had written poetry as a young person but hadn't written any more for years. However preposterous this proposition seemed to me, I decided to ponder it in my heart. Shortly after this, I decided to agree with what God had said to me and declared "Yes. I admit it, I'm a poet!" and cringed. Two weeks later, I reiterated those very words to a civic leader and was immediately put in charge of the entire poetry offering of a local festival of music and art!

As a result of that festival, I began to work with a concert pianist, writing poems inspired by the repertoire he chose and then performing them together with him in concert. I love seeing the satisfied response of audiences after each performance, as if we had just fed them a wonderful banquet of delightful, nourishing, exquisite food. I believe that the content and my delivery is good, it is truth, it is everything from my soul and it is me...but it is also Him. It isn't enough for me to create content myself, but to encourage others to do so as well I began to create radio programmes for the local radio station and encouraged other Christians to share their work, populating the radio waves with good quality and interesting content.

One of the people who attended my first Poetry and Piano performances invited me to come to the National Trust property that he managed and together we have established a very successful arts programme which has used arts to bring an ancient property to life. This opportunity led to my first publishing contract and I have been busy writing and performing poetry ever since with my hand in His!

Everyday, people are making new stuff. They're dreaming and walking out what their dreams are telling them; imagining and making those images, writing words, creating sounds and music, art and drama; they're capturing ideas and feeding them into channels of delivery through portals of concert halls, air waves and digital receptacles; printing on screens and paper; putting up pictures and photographs that cast atmospheres wherever they hang.

God wants Christians to be attending global forums like Davos and providing content for global platforms like ted.com, sharing our ideas and journeys–with eyes alight, burning with excitement, hope and passion. He wants the good news of faith, hope and love to get out through every possible means of authentic, transparent human expression.

FAMILY

Covenant relationships and personal identity, which are the key building blocks of society. Parenting styles, singleness, orphans, gender issues, marriage, sexuality, divorce, ageing, etc.

Camilla Douglas writes: Like Ginny, I can testify that it is still possible to be a culture changer in your

60s! Age is no barrier to having an adventure with God! Following a dramatic encounter with the Holy Spirit in 1994, I was "catapulted" into a new career with a small national charity called *Positive Parenting*, where I created resources for parents based on non–overt Christian principles.

Six years ago, God redirected my path towards neuroscience, after reading a ground–breaking book by Sue Gerhardt called *Why Love Matters: How Affection Shapes a Baby's Brain*. It showed that the "wiring" of the human brain is directly related to the kind of care the baby receives and the quality of his early relationships with parents and key carers. What I read seemed to hold the key to many of society's ills and was also compatible with Scripture. It was all about love! So, with the Holy Spirit's help and guidance, I have developed a range of visual resources called GroBrain focusing on bonding and brain development in babies. These materials are now being used effectively in the statutory sector.

However, the reality is that very few parents access parenting support in their child's formative years, at the very time when vital information is most needed. Christians have already been instrumental in developing initiatives such as Food Banks, CAP and Street Pastors. I believe we can do the same for parenting!

We are working on a new initiative (TotSlot), to deliver very short 'bite-sized' sessions on bonding at church-run parent and baby groups. This project has the potential to reach large numbers of parents and help change the culture. For more information please contact us via our website www.grobrain.co.uk.

ECONOMY

The system that produces, distributes and consumes wealth. Business, finance, management, social justice, capitalism, socialism, prosperity, poverty etc.

Edward Quicke writes: I came back to the Lord and was filled with the Holy Spirit aged 38, by which time I was a mid–career economist working in an international development organisation. I led multidisciplinary teams that evaluated and recommended loans to countries for projects in agriculture and rural development.

I was part of a group of Christians who met weekly for an early breakfast discussion, Bible study and prayer before starting work. Knowing Jesus' heart for the poor, one of the issues we discussed was how to lend to the poorest of the poor so that they could gain an income for themselves, when conventional bankers considered them not to be credit worthy. On one occasion, I invited the visionary chairman of a Christian micro–finance non–governmental organisation (NGO) to speak to this group. Over time, working with Governments and with input from some NGOs, we were able to get the conservative lending organisation for which I worked to finance some micro–finance projects. On the basis of their successful outcomes, an in–house specialist micro–finance unit was finally set up. I believe that it was partly due to that group of Christians, who met regularly for an early breakfast in the workplace, that such a radical shift in the organisation's lending policies was achieved.

FAITH

Faith and practice concerning what is ultimately true. Among the many voices on this mountain, the Church declares who God is and what Jesus has done to redeem creation.

Diana Chapman writes: I'm one of those Christians who falls into the category of someone who has been there, done it, got the T shirt, video...DVD and keeping up to date...the downloads AND not only lived to tell the tale but is still excited about Jesus and His church!

My formative years were in a Pentecostal church where the pastor was only a generation removed from the Welsh and Pentecostal revivals. Whilst at college I became an eager participant in the charismatic renewal. The "new church era" saw me in the numerous Dales, Wales and Downs Bible weeks and later hungrily throwing myself into the blessings from Heaven that flowed via Toronto. These years were punctuated by two years in a large "Faith Church" while living in Portugal and three years as a missionary in Africa.

Over 25 years ago I moved from the Education mountain where I was a schoolteacher, to the Religion mountain which I am still exploring to this day. Has it always been easy? No. When I came back to the UK from Africa in 2004 it was tough and I wrote in my journal that I wanted to be in a church that was thrilled by the presence of God, where the people were madly in love with Jesus and a place where the leadership were releasing and not controlling. The Holy Spirit led me to a Church in the Thames Valley where these are values we hold dear and with His help seek to live out.

For me, being in "church leadership" on the Religion Mountain, is not a hard climb to the top but a journey to be enjoyed with fellow "climbers." Where hierarchical structures give way to church based relationships mirroring the relationship between Father, Son and Spirit. Where in unity, identity is respected yet honour given and grace and love flows.

Recently, this phrase came into my mind, "Music and dancing are the sound of the Father's house." This was what the elder brother heard while he was in the field. The prodigal had returned and the Father had thrown a party. This led me to the challenging question, "What sounds do people hear from the church that will make them want to find out what is going on?"

As we explore life with Jesus, His company transforms us and, like the disciples on the road to Emmaus, our hearts burn within us. Bringing culture change in the religious mountain could be summed up from these verses I love in The Message: *"Are you tired? Worn out? Burned out on religion? Come to me. Get away with me and you'll recover your life. I'll show you how to take a real rest. Walk with me and work with me—watch how I do it. Learn the unforced rhythms of grace. I won't lay anything heavy or ill–fitting on you. Keep company with me and you'll learn to live freely and lightly."* Matthew 11:28–30

As we rest and learn to live our lives from Heavenly places in Christ Jesus, our perspective is shaped and opens up possibilities we would never consider from the valley. "On earth as it is in Heaven" becomes a reality to be lived and not just religious rhetoric. The impossible becomes possible and hope and faith are reborn.

I've said little about structure. That's because church is more about the new wine than the wineskins. About His presence rather than programmes. The container is functional only as it holds the wine and is able to pour it out. I believe that the God of creativity loves the diverse ways that His children build their "Bethels." Each are to be celebrated and respected.

FAMILY, BUSINESS, RELIGION

Jonathan Cavan, a family man, business entrepreneur writes:

I have been blessed with a wife who is an inspirational visionary in the creative arts, a son with a vocal range of 3.5 octaves designed to shift spiritual atmospheres and a daughter with a gift of dance that captivates hearts and releases Heaven. I have been blessed with a beautiful home in the Cotswolds in England and a God–given, profitable software business that affords me the time to make disciples who make disciples through an initiative called Lie Busters. I am a very blessed 50 year old man experiencing freedom and fruitfulness in many areas of my life...and it feels like just the beginning! But life hasn't always been this way so I'll attempt to share a little of my journey with you.

From slavery... Sadly, my bad genetic wiring combined with poor choices rendered me a very angry young man – a rebel without a pause! I had a competitive drive that wanted to win the human race and dominate others. In my twenties, I had a sex addiction and was taking alcohol and drugs daily, walking over people to prop up my derelict life. At the age of 29 my destructive drive had become more channeled into ambition and I had become Head of Corporate Sales at Microsoft UK. Outwardly my life looked good but inwardly it felt as though my cyclical behavioural patterns were strangling me to death. One night in 1991, I had a vision that led me into Holy Trinity Brompton, a church in London, where I had a radical conversion experience during which my whole body vibrated as I experienced the high voltage resonant frequency of Heaven. Soon thereafter, God led me to work at Microsoft HQ in the USA as Manager of Global Marketing Services where He set me up to witness to Bill Gates, Steve Ballmer and 500 senior executives around the world (this story can be found in the Alpha book called "The God Who Changes Lives Volume 1"). At the age of 31, I left Microsoft and did a full time BA in Biblical and Pastoral Studies back in the UK. I was an associate pastor for one year then realised that full–time paid ministry wasn't for me nor a model I could find in the New Testament so I went back into business whilst I continued to minister to the people God sent me.

To sonship: As a Christian I had many encounters with the Holy Spirit and Jesus really was my best friend, but I really didn't know God as my father. Like many other Christians, I was a spiritual orphan – meaning that I still had identity and authority issues and wasn't operating from a position of sonship. I wasn't ruling and reigning with Christ in Heavenly realms; I was very much earth–bound with an earthly perspective. After 17 years as a Christian this all changed in 2008, when I heard a talk by a young man called Chad Dedmon from Bethel Church in Redding, California. That night I had a vision that I was in the throne room in Heaven and God the Father was giving me a scroll which read, "Certificate of Sonship. You are my son, a light–bearing warrior. Your purpose is to displace darkness and declare freedom over nations, heal the sick and set captives free." Since that time EVERYTHING has changed. I have access to Heaven all the time and I have made declarations that have shifted principalities over nations. During 2,000+ hours of prayer ministry, I have witnessed many miracles including: a lady growing an inch; a knee ligament reconstructing and a mute speaking. I have cast out hundreds if not thousands of demons and seen many people enter sonship. I don't stress about finances and my business operates out of the abundant flow of Heaven. Words that describe my shift to sonship include IDENTITY, DESTINY, POWER and FLOW. As a son, I am far more relaxed about who I am.

To King maker: As Jesus is the King of Kings, we too are destined to be Kings, ruling and reigning on earth with Him from Heavenly places. I have learned that the ways of the Kingdom are opposite to the ways of the world. In the Kingdom of Heaven we are to serve in the natural and rule in the spiritual, whereas the enemy would have us rule over one another in the natural, thus serving him in the spiritual. As I learned to access Heaven as a son, my visions began to involve scenes of me as a King wearing a robe around my shoulders and a crown on my head. Many people are experiencing the same as a consequence of Lie Busting. Raising up the family of God has become my main mission in life; I take joy in sons and daughters of God ruling and reigning as Kings and Queens in their respective mountains of influence. I live to see the day when a whole generation will walk this earth as FREE sons and daughters of God. The following passage burns in my heart:

Romans 8:19: *"For the creation waits in eager expectation for the children of God to be revealed. ..... 21 that the creation itself will be liberated from its bondage to decay and brought into the freedom and glory of the children of God. 22 We know that the whole creation has been groaning as in the pains of childbirth right up to the present time. 23 Not only so, but we ourselves, who have the first fruits of the Spirit, groan inwardly as we wait eagerly for our adoption to sonship."*

In conclusion, I would say that I love family because it is the foundation and building block of God's government on earth. I love business because it is God's creative engine that generates resources for us all, and I love discipleship because it is God's plan to redeem humanity and transform the planet. The culture of all of these: family; business; and discipleship needs to change. I guess these values make me a Culture Changer and I'm very thankful that God has called Hugh and Ginny to connect other like minded people.

(Jonathan is married to Helena whose testimony is above. To connect with Lie Busters see their website : www.liebusters.org.)

GOVERNMENT

The system and policies by which we rule and are ruled. Politics, law, courts, taxes, prisons, military, bureaucracies, civic duty, activism, etc.

Jeremy Culverhouse writes: My vision straddles the mountains of Government and Business. I have always been an entrepreneur and marketplace minister, as Dr Bill Hamon says, "... the Church is wherever saints are functioning," and I believe that it is this Hebraic concept that eradicates the difference between ministry in the sanctuary and ministry in the world.

I want to see leaders come together, from both church and state, to transform cities across the world and see His Kingdom come on earth as it is in Heaven. I believe God is giving His people creative, innovative and socially transformative ideas to bring global communities together and to create wealth and opportunity, as a blessing from the Lord, which will act as a conduit for the Gospel.

"God impacts His city through corporate entities that He has envisioned; those corporate entities take land, they become landlords, and they govern the people by whatever those corporate rules are. Collectively all those corporate organisations can govern a city God's way," from *The Glory Returns to the Workplace* by Richard Fleming, 2004.

My Journey so far...

When I dreamt of leaving the City before retirement age, I had anticipated that it would be because I had made some money being a successful Broker. I had no idea what God was preparing me for or how He would choose to move in my life. So, when I was in my forties and my sixteen year old got pregnant, I nearly died from a burst colon, and false accusations wrecked my City career, the interruption of my nice middle class life was all something of a shock.

Having received words about being like Joseph since my twenties, I had largely ignored the fact that he experienced:– rejection from his family, was sold into slavery, thrown down a pit, falsely accused by a scheming woman and spent years in prison before he became Pharaoh's right hand man. In 2008, having crawled up out of the ruined career pit, I set up my own consultancy business, which was fruitful for a year until it became a victim of the global recession. All looked pretty bleak and my wife and I were desperate for some words of hope. So, in May 2009, we went to hear Isabel Allum, a woman with a mature prophetic gift, who had come to speak locally. She gave me another word about a Joseph anointing and that we were coming out of the season of the seven skinny cows and into the season of the seven fat cows. She also saw a set of house keys being given to us. It would surprise nobody who understands about how prophecy works that we then proceeded to have our beautiful brick and flint farmhouse repossessed, go bankrupt and spend the next three and a half years claiming benefits.

Since then God has arranged for me to be wined and dined by billionaires, make business connections to Arab Royalty, regularly go to the House of Lords and be part of the UK Global City Leaders Forum which has a mission to facilitate dialogue and city to city level connections between major city leaders (think Boris Johnson) in the UK and other parts of the world, starting with Manchester and some of China's second tier cities consisting of between 20 and 30 million people. And all this whilst still legitimately claiming Job Seekers Allowance ... rich or poor, I continue to run with the vision.

Sarah Culverhouse, married to Jeremy, writes: The Job Club. When we lost our income, our home and filed for bankruptcy, we began walking a path in the Benefits System which taught us what life on the bread line is truly like in Great Britain. We discovered that one of the greatest needs for job seekers was a friend to stand with them in finding work. So, supported by GB Job Clubs, a Christian charity, we began the Winchester

Job Club in July 2011.

We have since had the privilege of expressing the kindness of God in a practical way with countless people, some of whom only come once and we never see again. One woman we simply taught some basic interview techniques such as smiling at the interviewer. This so completely changed her confidence that the leader of Job Centre Plus said that our Job Club was being "transformational."

Job Centre Plus Staff were a huge support in that they constantly sign-posted people to come to us for CV writing, interview technique and online job searches. It's not rocket science; if you can write a CV and are confident with IT, you too could run a Job Club.

One of our favourite stories so far. A man came in full of bravado; he was a company director, and reeled out his CV which was very impressive, but then he slumped in his seat and said he had been unemployed for three years and it was a toss up that morning between coming to our Job Club or the Samaritans. My husband offered to pray for him, something we rarely do unless God opens a door, and he agreed. He then told my husband he had not prayed for twenty five years until 4am that very morning. Two weeks later he came back: God had given him a business idea and he wanted to tell us that the prayer had worked. Isn't God amazing?

And then there's the single mum, moved by Social

Services to our city as her partner broke her jaw, who told us she was pleased to be out of an environment where everyone just drank all day. She can barely read so can't do the Government's online Universal Job match. She doesn't say much but we picked her up on Sunday, drove her to our house and gave her a few hours off from her hostel room with two boisterous boys. We had lunch together and completed her online registration to the Job match. To us, THIS is expressing the love of the Father and the wonder of the Kingdom of God.

GOVERNMENT / PRISONS

GL – a prison chaplain writes: Every time I enter the prison, my main aim is to change the atmosphere of control and custody by bringing in the compassion and care of Jesus to the men who live there, all 1400 of them; and to the staff employed to care for them. There is nothing cosy or gentle in a prison regime, so I remind myself to put on the shoes of the gospel of peace (Ephesians 6) as I take the love of God into hostile places. The challenges are enormous, the emotions run high, the disappointments are frequent but so are the joys that shine through the day.

- The opportunity to pray with a man segregated for his own safety, who receives news of his young niece dying of cancer. To make the security arrangements for him to do what he feels is important which is to go to the chapel, light a candle and pray. He is not yet a believer but he is desperate for hope...we as chaplains can bring light and hope to these dark situations. No one has ever said "no" to being prayed for!

- The man receives a message from his mother because his ex-partner won't speak to him – that his baby is in hospital having been scalded. He is powerless and frantic. As a chaplain, I have the right to intervene and make the necessary calls to allay his fears and get the facts to him. His peace returns and life is bearable again, just.

- To visit and break news of a family death and to bear this with the prisoner.

- The joy of telling a man he has become a father and all is well.

I cannot over emphasise how important it is to bring the love of Jesus into this hostile environment, whether a day may be full of joys or sorrows. As a chaplain, I have the ability and the authority to walk with peace, hope and love down these dark corridors.

GOVERNMENT / MILITARY

RR – a soldier writes : My experiences in the Armed Forces have brought me to understand the pain and suffering that today's soldiers are going through. That rather than ignoring their problems, we, as **Culture Changers**, should be there in the flesh for them. We are to stand alongside them, guiding them through the traumas and nightmares; to be a rock for them to cling to as their wounds heal. I have met with many soldiers returning from theatres of conflict, have listened to their fears, sat with them through their nightmares and tried to give them reason to carry on – by being there for them. A soldier is a person who lives life by fact not fiction (their lives depend on it). So by sharing the truth of how much God loves us they can receive the abundance of all that God has for them.

EDUCATION

Who, what, when, where, why and how we teach the next generation. Public and private schools, textbooks, literacy, indoctrination versus education, universities etc.

Deputy Head Teacher writes: I never thought I would be a teacher. However, after three years of publishing lots of books, my wife and I started to run a youth club and a children's holiday play–scheme through our local church. I realised this was something I enjoyed, could do and what's more, be paid for it! Each day, as I crossed Waterloo Bridge to work, I said to God "Shall I become a teacher?" His clear response was "Go into teaching and I will be with you." And He has been with me. And so much more! He has constantly sustained me over twenty years of work alongside bringing up our four boys.

I've treated teaching as much like daily social work as teaching educational skills, much to the irritation of some advisors and inspectors. It is summed up when I see troubled nine-year-old eyes and I ask God to show me the problem.

Not long ago, a teacher asked for advice about a girl who had been stealing things from the class. In this case, it was chocolate that had been given to them by a parent to share. The teacher wanted to give the girl a strict telling off and a punishment, but I suggested sitting the girl down to talk it over. God showed me the trouble as she spoke. She felt no sense of value and stealing had become a compulsive habit. I reassured the girl how important she was to us and to her friends and she broke down in tears. I then said she would have to put it right by owning up to her class. She did it, brave girl, and they clearly forgave her. At this point she turned to her best friend and admitted stealing some other things from her too! "Don't worry", said the other girl, giving her a hug. Repentance and then forgiveness from her friends brought real restoration. The teacher was amazed at the process she witnessed.

For me, God's order for muddled lives is so very worthwhile. Teaching has a rhythm; it is always busy in term time, often frustrating but never boring. The holidays bring rest and time to be imaginative again so that planning is inspired and not dull. The children deserve our best.

I have taught for 17 years in state schools and 4 years in an independent school. You experience the results of people's lives; families with multiple fathers, parents who have gone through sex changes, children who are consistently moving home and school, those whose first language is not English, overly busy career parents. In my response to this, I am not allowed to share my faith openly. However, I can ask God's help to honour the children in my care and I believe this has a huge effect. As a leader within the school, living a life of integrity means resolving complicated, emotional disagreements between staff in a way that also honours and gives the opportunity for restoration.

The need to soften one's heart and forgive others is a daily necessity. Remembering that, *"Our battle is not against flesh and blood (people) but against the rulers, against the authorities, against the powers of this dark world and against the spiritual forces of evil in the Heavenly realms"* Ephesians 6 has led me into an active intercessory life. It is tempting to battle people, but we are to love the people and battle, in prayer, the spirit behind the harmful words or action. I have regularly had to pray to break strongholds of manipulation and control, fear, destruction and division before going into school, and found this to impact and transform frustrating situations.

I have also learnt to let God be the judge of all people, particularly when at times you are misrepresented, lied about and misunderstood. We can't put everything right but we can leave all things with our God of justice, standing firm in our given Heavenly authority. My calling is to love, value and forgive everyone.

SCIENCE AND TECHNOLOGY

Our knowledge of creation and how we practically apply it. Health, medicine, innovation, sanitation, the printing press, computers, weaponry etc.

Dr. Kate Jutsum, working in an Accident and Emergency Department writes: God and medicine has been, and still is, a journey for me. There has long been a school of thought in the church that those who are educated cannot access the Holy Spirit in His fullness. And that, in the scientific world, a real scientist would not waste time or space on the spiritual. Being an Emergency doctor and encountering people who need emotional and spiritual healing, not just drugs and quick fixes, has shown me what warped science can look like.

115

Equally, through my involvement in healing ministry, I encounter some people with a warped spirituality, who need to go to a doctor for medical help but refuse to do so on the basis of their "faith." Neither is pretty, because actually science is a study of the mind of God – spirituality and science belong together. There is no sacred–secular divide. Having realised and accepted that my place is in the middle of this tension my heart is to see God and medicine flowing so closely together that one is not distinguishable from the other. The person is just healed as God flows through a professional excellent in their field and surrendered to His leading.

Early on my Emergency bosses informed me that I was not to mention God or church to my patients. I found this to be a sentence that squeezed life out of me every day as I saw many people's real needs to be love and hope rather than drugs. At my wits' end and forbidden to give this love openly, I prayed "God, if you do not do something, I'm leaving medicine. I just can't do this any longer."

His words to me changed everything. "Don't you realise darkness attracts my light." In losing hope, I'd also lost my impact in a pain, grief and chaos filled place. So I started to ask God how He saw my Department and spent time choosing to agree with Him, rather than agreeing with the inferior "reality" around me. I'd always silently prayed for every patient I got my hands on, but now started to walk in to the Department intentionally carrying hope, releasing an atmosphere of peace and joy and raising a standard for righteousness. Within two weeks my immediate surroundings changed; I was loving my job again and broke into clearer thought, more efficient work, better treatment of patients and ease. Staff started smiling when I came in "Oh you're here – the day just got so much better." A few weeks later I was in charge of the Department on one of the busiest weekends of the year – School Sports Finals Day! As the day progressed we were predictably busy, with the normal weekend workload – DIY and sporting accidents, GP patients, cardiac and trauma cases, plus a load of children and young adults from the Sports Finals. We were run off our feet. But the atmosphere in that place was incredible – it felt like Christmas! The usual chaos, anxiety and darkness had been replaced by a sense of settled happiness. When the nurse in charge pulled me aside into an empty resuscitation bay at the end of my shift I thought it was to notify me of a trauma about to arrive. However, instead, she handed me a box of chocolates and thanked me "for making this such an easy day to work." Her report noted how peaceful and easy that day had been, despite the number of patients, and ascribed full credit to me for the situation. That day was a turnaround day for me. There really is no place that God cannot invade with His goodness.

WE ARE ALL WORLD CHANGERS!

We believe that, as sons and daughters walking out our destiny, we are empowered by the Holy Spirit to rule and reign in our spheres of influence. In this way, His glory will be carried to the ends of the earth as we all fulfil our calling to be a contributor to the societies in which we live. Our call is to honour both those in authority and those in our society who are not recognised as successful.

We all have the potential to be world changers! James Hudson Taylor, the great pioneer and reformer, describes this work brilliantly. He says **"We are a supernatural people, born again by a supernatural birth; we wage a supernatural fight and are taught by a supernatural teacher, led by a supernatural captain to assured victory."** This is the normal Christian life we are called to. Expecting the supernatural to be part of our spirit filled lives, relishing what each day will bring and sharing with one another what God has been doing amongst us all. Standing against injustice and not being ignorant of the enemy's schemes.

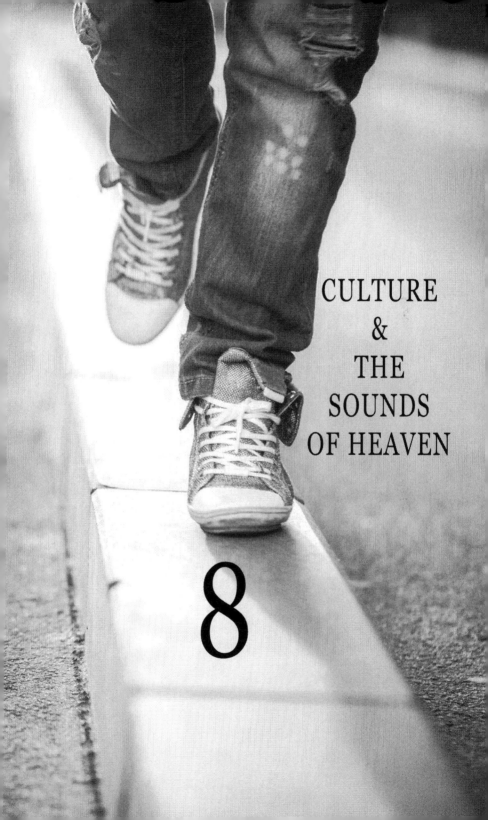

CULTURE
&
THE
SOUNDS
OF HEAVEN

8

Chapter Eight

CULTURE & THE SOUNDS OF HEAVEN

Faith Blatchford

Recognising that we each have a unique destiny, we realise that no one else can fulfil our call! Illustrating this, Faith Blatchford writes this concluding chapter. A woman of great faith, her comments will spur us on to be all that our Heavenly Dad has destined each one of us to be. She writes:

CATACLYSMIC CHANGE

A quick glance at headlines brings an immediate realisation that society is rapidly changing. It feels as if a huge avalanche is free–falling, gathering speed, soon to envelop the world as we know it. The challenge to believers is the momentum of this cataclysmic event as it moves in opposition to the advancing Kingdom of God.

Some of us want to jump headlong into the midst of the moving mountain of snow and yell, "Stop!" Others are more hesitant, feeling they aren't powerful enough to stop the avalanche. The truth is, we are all affecting our world whether we try to stop this momentum or not. The issue is – what kind of culture are we creating? Are we bringing about godly changes or adding to the decline?

COLLISION OF CULTURES

The Bible repeatedly describes this clash of kingdoms and this collision of cultures. The Paradise of Eden came under assault in the Garden as the serpent persuaded Eve to doubt the benevolence of her creator. Moses stood his ground, representing the Kingdom of God in the court of Pharaoh against the sorcerers, the power brokers of Egypt. The Old Testament is the history of the endless cycle of Kingdom advance and decline throughout the ages.

Jesus appeared on the stage of history in the midst of another period of decline. The morals and behaviour of the world of His day were more obscene and x-rated than those in the 21st century. In the midst of ungodliness, greed, lust, murder, violence, abortion and slavery, Jesus told his disciples in Luke 11:2 to pray "thy Kingdom come on earth as it is in Heaven." Furthermore, He commanded them in Matthew 28:9

to "make disciples of all nations." This command was given to an impoverished, dis-empowered small group of people in a country that would be considered Third World today.

FOLLOWERS OF JESUS
CULTURAL CHANGE AGENTS

Yet, we read in Acts 17:6 that these same disciples had "turned the world upside down." The reverberations of their activity are still being felt today. The ministry of Jesus, represented by his disciples, radically changed the course of history, touching every aspect of culture, including government, entertainment, family values, finance, religion, education and the arts.

"Jesus had a birthday and that birthday utterly altered the way we measure time." So writes James Kennedy in his book, What If Jesus Had Never Been Born? That one day marked the shift in the calendar from B.C. (before Christ) to A.D. (Anno Domini— in the year of The Lord). Today we are faced with another period of decline. The vision of **Culture Changers** is not merely to create safe, free, gathering places for believers, but also to bring transformation to society so that it looks, feels, and acts like Heaven. Sounds wonderful, but how do we do it?

Romans 1:30 paints a clear picture of a corrupt society, filled with "all unrighteousness, fornication, wickedness, covetousness, maliciousness; full of envy, murder, debate, deceit, malignity; whisperers, backbiters, haters of God, despiteful, proud, boasters, inventors of evil, disobedient to parents, without understanding, covenant breakers, without natural affection, implacable, unmerciful." Sounds familiar?

Often, the focus of religion has been to deal with all those symptoms in order to reform society. Through the use of guilt, shame, ostracism, punishment, and laws, it has sought to restore holiness and the Kingdom of Heaven on earth without addressing the root issue.

KEYS TO CULTURAL TRANSFORMATION

The secret of cultural transformation is two–fold. First, men and women must be reintroduced to their glorious God. Once they meet the true God, they will glorify Him with thanksgiving and be transformed in their minds, hearts and behaviour from glory to glory.

As **Culture Changers**, our call is to obey Jesus' command in Matthew 5:16 when He said: "Let your light so shine before men that they may see your good works and glorify your Father which is in Heaven." The "good works" were the supernatural signs and wonders done through the disciples by the Holy Spirit. These good works meant healing the sick, opening blind eyes and deaf ears, casting out demons, raising the dead, preaching the good news to the poor. This supernatural activity of the Holy Spirit is the fire around which the Church gathers together to worship. Jesus told the woman at the well the Father was looking for worshippers who would worship Him in Spirit and in truth.

WORSHIP AND REVIVAL HISTORY

Reading through the pages of church history is like looking through an enormous hymnbook. From the Old Testament days of David, the Psalm writer, through every great revival, worship has been a hallmark of the presence of God among His people. Each period of revival had particular songs, hymns, choruses that drew the presence of God. People attending those meetings remember feeling the Holy Spirit moving as the congregations sang specific songs. Equally, bringing Heaven to earth means releasing not only supernatural health, wholeness, purity, abundance, provision and the fellowship of Heaven, but also the sounds. The book of Revelation pulls back the curtain of the throne room, revealing men and women from every tribe and tongue joined together in worship – Heaven's health being immersed in ceaseless praise.

UNEXPECTED HEALING
THROUGH PRAISE

I heard the testimony of a man who was terminally ill with a lung disease. He had been given three months to live. The realisation of his short time left on earth caused him to do a spiritual inventory to get his affairs in order and restore any broken relationships. As he knew his life in Heaven would involve continuous worship and praise, he decided to spend his days getting ready for his place in Heaven's choir by singing and giving thanks to God every day, learning how to be a worshipper.

Over the next weeks and months he discovered he was feeling a little better and able to breathe more freely. At the end of the three months, his doctor gave him incredible news. They found no trace of the illness left in his lungs. Although his focus had been on worship, not physical restoration, he was totally healed as he identified with Heaven's atmosphere of worship.

THE MAGNET THAT BRINGS
HEAVEN TO EARTH

Our vision is for **Culture Changers** families around the world to be known for love, joy, and miracles, as well as the sounds of Heaven rising in the atmosphere from our worship, bringing the blessings of Heaven to earth. As more people experience supernatural encounters with the Father, the resulting worship will begin to reverse the sickness of our culture. Healing and the restoration of society will take place as men and women are transformed in their minds and their behaviour through their worship of God. The atmosphere changes because praise is a magnet, which draws Him. Psalm 22:3 says God inhabits the praises of His people. The culture of the earth changes when He comes, perhaps even in an instant, because where He is, Heaven is.[1]

EndNotes

1 Faith's Resources:
    Faith Blatchford – www.faithblatchford.com
    Ray Hughes – www.selahministries.com
    Dan McCollam – www.ibethel.org/users/
    danmccollam

Culture Changers... Reconnecting His Family

RESOURCES

9

Culture Changers... Reconnecting His Family

chapter nine

RESOURCES

God loves His whole church and so do we. We remember that men do not pour new wine into old wineskins. If they do the skins will burst, the wine will run out and the wineskins will be ruined, therefore they pour new wine into new wineskins and both are preserved.

If you would like to connect with the growing Culture Changing Family then go to "connect" on our website: www.culture-changers.org You will then receive a monthly update and also have the opportunity to meet up with others like yourselves whether living locally to you – or via the internet.

The following ministries represent friends who have stood with us on this journey. Their websites will give you resources that might help you in a host of different ways.

Catch the Fire
http://resources.catchthefire.com

Global Awakening
http://globalawakeningstore.com

Bethel Church, Redding, California
http://store.ibethel.org

Global Legacy
http://store.igloballegacy.org

Steve and Wendy Backlund
http://www.ignitedhope.com

Faith Blatchford – Creativity sozo
http://www.faithblatchford.com

Vineyard – John Wimber
http://www.vineyard.org

Quaker – George Fox
http://www.quaker.org

Re–vived
http://www.re–vived.com

Kingdom Writing Solutions
http://www.kingdomwritingsolutions.org

Jesus Ministry
http://www.sycamorepublications.com

Communion with God
http://www.cwgministries.org/

La Red
http://www.lared.org/

Life Stream Ministries
http://www.lifestream.org

Lie Busters
http://www.liebusters.org

Joining the Dots
https://www.joiningthedotsdistribution.co.uk

CHILDREN'S RESOURCES

Power Pack Ministries
http://www.powerpackministries.co.uk/

What is in the Bible
http://whatsinthebible.com/

Jelly Telly
http://www.jellytelly.com/

The Jesus Story book
http://zondervan.com/9780310708254

Appendix One

BELONGING AND BELIEVING

Going to church can be a natural thing – but following Jesus is a supernatural thing! There is a world of difference between the two. The Bible is full of supernatural accounts of God meeting with His people, His family, and demonstrating His great love and power for them.

Once we start turning towards God we are always welcome in His family. However, there is a point at which one wants to actually belong oneself. A way of walking through the gate rather than jumping over the fence! This chapter is particularly for those who are picking up this book and finding out how they can become a family member rather than just remaining a friend!! You might say a "rite of passage" – and yes – there is always room for us! It is almost impossible to explain spiritual things but here goes:

ENDING THE SLAVE TRADE!

Nobody is perfect. Indeed sometimes we seem to be slaves to the things that deep down we know are wrong. The Bible calls these things "sin" and tells us that they separate us from God. The truth is that we all fall short and we all need help. Our Heavenly Father loves us but knows that the sin in our lives prevents us from really "living" life at its best. Like any good father, He wants to liberate us. Therefore He made a way for our sins to be forgiven so that we may become part of His family and live life to the full.

Before I share His rescue plan, we need to be aware that there are two teams on the field. The first team belongs to our Heavenly Father and the other to our enemy, satan, who delights in the fact that we are enslaved to our sins. He approaches us with malicious intent, looking to steal, slaughter and destroy, but God's son, Jesus, comes to give us life with joy and abundance. The Bible reminds us that we are not to be unaware of the enemy's schemes or his power – but neither are we to focus on them. Whilst our enemy, the devil, can't get a single blow in while God is not looking – we have the choice of joining or leaving either team. The winning team far outweighs the losing team – but the enemy's team does a lot of advertising!

To release ourselves from the enemy's grip requires three things: God's kindness, our repentance and a mediator between us. As we experience the goodness of

God and recognise that He loves us for who we are and not for what we do – or even for what we might become – so we want a relationship with Him even more! For this to happen we need to repent. This is not a fear–induced decision but comes from a new longing in our heart for a second chance. Repentance is the ticket for our return journey back to the heart of God. It is a response to God not an act that earns a reward!

Jesus is our Mediator. His mission with a purpose deals with the punishment we deserve for our sins. He takes our place and "in God's eyes pays for them" by allowing Himself to be executed in our place on the cross. He laid down His life to be crucified for us. In that sacrificial act, as He bled and died in agony for each of us – He made restitution for our sins and changed our destination from hell to Heaven. It would be an understatement to call this "the great exchange"! As we repent and accept that this costly mission was for us – so we are restored into God's family. A simple plan, although given at great cost, where we actually become "saints" rather than "sinners"!

I love the way Bob Goff puts it: "A couple of other things happen when we accept Jesus' invitation to participate with Him in life. Obstacles that seem insurmountable aren't! Impediments that we believe disqualify us don't! When we show up to participate with Jesus in the big life, we are participating with the very being who made life in the first place. He gently asks us how we are and invites us to get better together with Him."

When we accept this invitation, it is contagious! Other people will watch us and start seeing life as something more amazing, more whimsical than before. People don't think about their pain or their weakness any longer.1 Instead, they think about how incredible this new life is and how powerful their Heavenly father is too.

A WORLD WHERE LOVE
IS THE FOUNDATION

The Bible calls this transaction "being born again." We are rescued out of the dominion of darkness and brought into the Kingdom of God. Suddenly we find that a part of us that we had not recognised before comes alive. It is as though we have found something we have always longed for, yet never knew the way in. Although we are fully human, our spirit is now ignited and we feel different. This is because we are now a spirit being in a world where love is the foundation. We become part of a family whose father receives, accepts and loves us for who we are and not how we perform. A father who wants a genuine, kind, personal, intimate relationship with us. A place where we belong.

So what is our new Dad like? He is a loving, approachable father – not "the big policeman in the sky!" Furthermore, He is part of an equally amazing Heavenly family where His Son also loves us and His Holy Spirit is there to guide us.

CONNECTIVITY

But that is not all! For years many people thought that being forgiven was the whole package for those who follow Jesus. As awesome as it is to now be free from guilt, fear, control and life's general mess, there is much more! Like a good earthly Dad, our Father in Heaven wants to share all He has with us. As well as forgiving us our sins, He opens the way for connectivity rather than loneliness, enabling us to enjoy our true identities as His sons and daughters. Our relationships with Him and with one another are now our top priority. When our spirits are re–connected to our loving, Heavenly Dad, we feel deeply safe and secure as children of the living God, confident and trusting in Him. We learn to live as members of His family – watching how He does things and then doing the same things ourselves.

To be included in His Family, Jesus tells us to repent, believe and then be baptised in water straight away! The following prayer may be helpful as you begin to take these steps:

"Lord Jesus, Please forgive me for the things I have done wrong in my life (take as long as you like in telling Him what these things are). Thank you for paying for my sins and embracing abandonment for me by dying on the cross. I now turn from my sins and from everything which I know is wrong.

Thank you that I am now forgiven and set free. Thank you that I have become a member of Your family and that I am no longer a spiritual orphan

I am now your son/daughter and part of your family on earth as it is in Heaven. Please daily fill me with your Holy Spirit, bring the Bible alive to me and connect me with others in Your family. Thank you."

It is important now to connect with your new brothers and sisters for love and support. They will help you follow Jesus (this is discipleship) which will include wanting to read the Bible and inviting the Holy Spirit into your life as you learn to walk with Him and seek His guidance.

EndNotes

1 From *Love Does* by Bob Goff

Appendix Two

HEALING DECLARATIONS

These declarations can be used daily as part of the armoury to protect us from disease and infirmity. We can remind ourselves that we are redeemed from the curse of the law, therefore illness or disease is illegal in our bodies and we do not give them any authority to stay. These declarations have been a great blessing to me and I hope they might be to you – or to someone you know who has battled, or is battling with a life defining illness. We are to stand and fight knowing that faith comes by hearing not just by thinking (Romans 10:17). Therefore these words need to be spoken out loud.

1. Since Jesus is Lord over my life, I forbid sin, sickness, and disease to have any power over me. I am forgiven and free from sin and guilt. I am dead to sin and alive unto the righteousness of God. (Colossians 1:21–22).

2. The Word of God has imparted the life of God to me, and that life restores my body with every breath I breathe and every word I speak. I overcome the world, the flesh, and the devil by the blood of the

Lamb and the word of my testimony (John 6:63; Mark 11:23; 1 John 4:4; Revelation 12:11).

3. Jesus bore my sickness and carried my pain; therefore, I give no place to sickness and pain, for God sent His Word and healed me and delivered me from the pit of destruction (Psalms 107:20; Ecclesiastes 10:11).

4. Heavenly Father, I attend to Your Word; I incline my ears to Your sayings; I refuse to let them depart from my eyes, I keep them in the midst of my heart for they are life, health, and medicine to all my flesh (Proverbs 4:20–22).

5. You have given me abundant life and I receive that life through Your Word; and that life flows to every organ and tissue of my body, bringing life and health (John 10:10; John 6:63).

6. Father, I am redeemed from the curse and Your eternal life is in me, Your Word, which is eternal life, flows in my blood stream, restoring every cell of my body to health, in Jesus' name (John 6:8; John 10:28; 1 John 5:11, 13–15, 20).

7. Lord, I serve You and You bless my food and water and You have taken sickness out of me; therefore, I will fulfil the number of my days on the earth in health (Exodus 23:25–26).

8. Since my body is the temple of the Holy Spirit, my body releases the perfect chemical balance. My pancreas secretes the right amount of insulin for life and health (1 Corinthians 6:19).

9. I am redeemed from the curse of the law; therefore, I forbid growths, tumours, blood diseases, heart malfunctions, cancers, strokes, arthritis, high blood pressure, or any sickness or disease of any kind to inhabit my body; I am delivered out of the authority of darkness and every organ and tissue of my body functions in the perfection to which God has created it to function (Galatians 3:13; Colossians 1:13–14; Genesis 1:28–31).

10. I speak to my blood; I command every red and white cell to destroy every diseased germ, virus, or alien cell that is trying to inhabit my body. In Jesus' name, I command every cell of my body to be made normal and I forbid any malfunction in my body cells (Mark 11:23; Luke 17:6; 1 John 5:14–15).

11. Every foreign cell that is not promoting life and health in my body is cut off from its life source. My blood cells will not allow one abnormal cell or tumorous growth to live in my body (Luke 17:6; 1 John 5:14–15).

12. I speak to my blood, my bones, my marrow, my joints, and every internal organ, and I call you

normal, in Jesus' name. My bones and joints will not respond to any disease. I speak to pain, swelling and inflammation, and I command you to line up with God's word. God sent his word and healed me and delivered me from every disease, sickness, infirmity, and every pit of destruction, for Jesus is my Healer (Psalms 107:20).

13. Body, I speak the word of faith to you. I command every internal organ to perform a perfect work, for you are the temple of the Holy Ghost. I charge you, in the name of the Lord Jesus Christ and by the authority of His holy word, to be healed and made whole. (Proverbs 12:13; 1 Corinthians 3:16–17, 6:19; 1 John 5:14–15)

14. I command my bones to produce perfect marrow; I command my marrow to produce pure blood that will ward off sickness and disease. My bones refuse any offence of the curse. (Proverbs 16:24; 1 John 5:14–15)

15. Father, as I give voice to Your word, the law of the Spirit of life in Christ Jesus makes me free from the law of sin and death. Your life is energising every cell of my body (Romans 8:2).

16. I resist the enemy in every form that he takes as he comes against me. I require my body to be strong and healthy and I enforce it with Your word. I reject

the curse and I enforce life in this body. I will not die but live and declare the works of God (John 4:7; Psalms 118;17).

Appendix Three

BOB JONES' PROPHECY

This prophecy, given on 25th February 2011, is about keys being released to bring about change in leadership, church structure and the true identity of his people that will lead to new realms of glory. You may locate it at the website in the endnote.[1]

"Jesus is giving keys to the mothers and fathers of the faith to unlock the Kingdom of God in others that will enable them to make a great advance. God desires to unlock the Kingdom in His people to bring forth the Kingdom of Heaven through His people. The keys that God is releasing will also bring about change in leadership, church structure and the true identity of His people that will lead to new realms of glory. Change will take place as God's people are established in their true identity to possess their ordained inheritance as sons and daughters of the King as citizens of His Kingdom."

When the spirit of a man connects with His creator who is a Spirit, the spirit of a person comes alive with the Spirit of God. It doesn't matter how long they have been a Christian, this experience "shifts" them from the

147

natural to the supernatural realm before your very eyes. As their spirit is released to the throne of God, the light, life and glory of God touches them and awakens them to their destiny. This experience is life changing. What takes place is an infusion of the light, life and love of God that remains with them. You can see the light come into their eyes as their countenance changes. In other words, they own it and as they walk in His light, His glory becomes their spiritual reality not just a Biblical theology.

God is raising up mothers and fathers with the key to awaken hearts that will enable them to see who they really are so they can from their place of true identity, step into the place of their purpose with Kingdom authority. It is only when the eyes of our hearts are opened to see how God has created us in His image and positioned us as citizens of the Kingdom that we can understand who we really are. Our true identity is not in what we do, but in our being! Who we are is more important than what we do!

EndNotes

1 http://www.bobjones.org

About The Author

After being dramatically converted and filled with the Holy Spirit, Ginny and her husband Hugh joined the emerging Vineyard Movement in 1987. Seven years later they planted the Winchester Vineyard –  the church they love deeply and to whom they became a father and mother. In 2011 they handed the 'Winvin' over to wonderful successors and a new journey began to unfold for them. To their great surprise, they were sovereignly and supernaturally called to leave denominationalism and pursue a vision to see God's family reconnected. A defender of the weak, a mother and grandmother, a teacher, a leader and a visionary, Ginny is passionate to see the Kingdom come "on earth as it is in Heaven."

Culture Changers... Reconnecting His Family

Culture Changers
...owing the World an encounter with a Good God

To connect with us go to

www.culture-changers.org
info@culture-changers.org

Culture Changers is a Charitable Company, Registered in England and Wales.
Company No. 8268325 and Charity No. 1152979

Culture Changers... Reconnecting His Family